[*Photograph by A. W. Kerr.*
LT.-COL. R. L. HAINE, V.C., M.C., at Saluting Base with LT.-COL. A. J. CHAPMAN and Chairman of Coulsdon and Purley Urban District Council.

A History

of the

58th Surrey Battalion Home Guard

◆

by
W. C. Dodkins

◆

With a foreword by
Col. Ambrose Keevil,
C.B.E., M.C., D.L.

◆

The Naval & Military Press Ltd

Published by

The Naval & Military Press Ltd
Unit 10 Ridgewood Industrial Park,
Uckfield, East Sussex,
TN22 5QE England

Tel: +44 (0) 1825 749494
Fax: +44 (0) 1825 765701

www.naval-military-press.com
www.nmarchive.com

In reprinting in facsimile from the original, any imperfections are inevitably reproduced and the quality may fall short of modern type and cartographic standards.

Although the British military position is so hopeless, they show not the slightest sign of giving in

> Extract from Original Nazi plan for the invasion of England initialled by KEITEL, former Chief of the High Command, and JODL, former Chief of Army Operations.

Contents

	Page
THE BIRTH OF THE L.D.V.	1
COMMANDERS ARE APPOINTED	4
REMINISCENCES OF 1940	8
THE NIGHTLY DUTIES	12
THE BATTALION TAKES SHAPE	15
THE HOME GUARD "OTHER RANKS"	20
FROM DEFENSIVE TO OFFENSIVE	22
HOME GUARD WEAPONS	27
BATTLE INOCULATION AND EXERCISES WITH REGULAR ARMY	30
THE HOME GUARD OFFICER	33
THE BOYS OF THE 58TH	36
1944—THE LAST YEAR OF EMBODIED SERVICE	38
1945—THE YEAR OF VICTORY	46
"AMONG MEN"	49
Contributed by Companies—	
"A" COMPANY	50
"B" COMPANY	52
"C" and "D" COMPANIES	54
HEADQUARTERS COMPANY AND MOBILE RESERVE	61
"THE HOME GUARD"	64
NOMINAL ROLL OF THE BATTALION	66
NOMINAL ROLL OF WOMEN AUXILIARIES	80

Illustrations

Lt.-Col. R. L. Haine, v.c., m.c., at the Saluting Base with Lt.-Col. A. J. Chapman and the Chairman of the Coulsdon and Purley Urban District Council	*Frontispiece*
Major-General H. G. Anderson, c.b., c.m.g., d.s.o.	*facing page* 4
Local Defence Volunteers, 1940 . . .	*facing page* 8
Colonel Ambrose Keevil, c.b.e., m.c., d.l.	*facing page* 16
On Bisley Ranges	*facing page* 28
In the Bombing Bay	*facing page* 32
As the Home Guard Stand Down Hitler's Volkssturm Stand To . . .	*facing page* 44
"A" Company on the march at Carshalton, May, 1943	*facing page* 50
"B" Company Parade at Woodcote Village Green	*facing page* 52
"C" Company give a Demonstration . .	*facing page* 54
"D" Company's Inspection at Kenley, May, 1941	*facing page* 58
Mobile Reserve—The "King's" Detachment .	*facing page* 62
Officers of the 58th at "Stand Down" . .	*facing page* 65

Foreword

by Col. Ambrose Keevil, C.B.E., M.C., D.L.

WHEN, AFTER THE BROADCAST APPEAL for Local Defence Volunteers on the night of May 14th, 1940, I took my place in the queue of men eager to join, I little thought I should have the honour of commanding "Z" Zone of that great citizen army from May, 1942, until it was disbanded at the end of 1945.

Major Dodkins has told the story of the 58th Surrey in which he served, but his little book should have a wider appeal as he has been successful in describing, not only a record of events, but something of the wonderful spirit of comradeship and service to the community which animated the Home Guard from the outset. No one can question the truth of his words, that if the spirit of SERVICE NOT SELF prevailed throughout the world to-day many problems which now beset us would be remedied or solved.

"Z" Zone consisted of many different formations, and although comparisons are impossible I can with all sincerity say the 58th was second to none. It was a fine Battalion in which I had complete confidence, and, for its Officers and other ranks, a great personal admiration and friendship.

AMBROSE KEEVIL.

May 14th, 1948.

Introduction

THIS IS A BRIEF HISTORY of a General Service Battalion of the Home Guard, a force which, as Local Defence Volunteers, was brought into being during the Second World War, 1939-1945, at a time when Britain stood alone.

In its early days the Battalion consisted mostly of men who had served in the First World War, 1914-1918, veterans of the Royal Navy, of Mons, Ypres, the Somme, Passchendale, and Gallipoli. A few wore the ribbons of the South African War, 1899-1902, and occasionally was noticed a ribbon of an even earlier war, although the age given by its wearer upon enrolment denoted that he must have been a baby in arms at the time.

The area from which the Battalion was recruited suffered considerably from aerial bombardment, but the story of the "blitz" has been told elsewhere. This is merely a short account of the raising, organising, and training, of one of the thousand and eighty-four battalions of that great citizen army formed to deal with any attempt at invasion.

To record the Battalion's activities over a period of four-and-a-half years is easier than to do justice to its members' enthusiasm. Young or old, they trained hard to fit themselves for the defence of their country and would have given their lives to that end. No call was ever made upon them to which they did not willingly respond, and had the threatened invasion taken place, they would have done their best to uphold the traditions of the British people.

CHAPTER ONE
The Birth of the L.D.V.

THE HISTORY OF ANY BATTALION of the Home Guard can begin in only one way—with the appeal made by Mr. Anthony Eden, then Minister for War in Mr. Churchill's newly-formed Government, in a broadcast after the nine o'clock news on the night of May 14th, 1940, five days after the first bombs on the mainland of Britain for twenty-two years had fallen near Canterbury. He announced the formation of a force to be known as the Local Defence Volunteers, which, in uniform and with arms, but without pay, would help to protect the country from the menace of paratroops. Men between the ages of seventeen and sixty-five, willing to take up arms in their country's defence, were to apply at the nearest police station.

When that appeal was made things were going badly for Britain. Denmark and Norway had been invaded and Holland over-run. Heavily armed enemy paratroops, dropped behind the lines in Holland and Belgium, sometimes in Allied uniforms or civilian clothes, caused panic and confusion. The German hordes, bursting through the Ardennes valleys, had crossed the River Meuse and overwhelmed the French Ninth Army. The right flank of the British Expeditionary Force was threatened, although how seriously was not then realised, but in fact the famous retreat to Dunkirk was about to begin. Within a fortnight the Belgians capitulated and the British were fighting their way to the coast. In just over a fortnight the evacuation was complete and the Germans masters of Europe. We stood alone!

No sooner was the wireless appeal made than men thronged the police stations all over the country. Young men eager for action, older men who had fought in other wars and waited impatiently for their country's call; men of all classes, trades, and professions. Whoever or whatever they were in civil life, one thing they shared in common—a grim determination to save their country from the fate that had overtaken Europe.

At the police stations in the locality harassed police officers took particulars and helped applicants to fill up forms; until late that night they answered innumerable questions, did the same the following morning as the queues began to assemble at an early hour, and many mornings after that. Each applicant was told he would be notified where and when to attend for enrolment. All through those early days the police acted as "father" to the newly-formed L.D.V. and this spirit of friendship and co-operation was maintained to the end.

Meanwhile certain prominent local men had been entrusted with the task of enrolling and organising these L.D.V's into what were called "Zones". In the Metropolitan Police District each Divisional area became a Zone for the L.D.V. and took the same distinguishing letter. Consequently "Z" Zone, with its headquarters at Croydon, included L.D.V's in Carshalton, Wallington, Coulsdon, Purley, Kenley and Whyteleafe (the area of the Purley Battalion) as well as other adjacent boroughs. Each Zone organiser had under him a number of Group or sub-Zone organisers.

The creator of "Z" Zone was the late Major N. Gillett, who for many years had been Clerk to the Croydon Justices. Not only did he possess a thorough knowledge of the locality but also considerable military experience, for as a pre-1914 Territorial Officer, he mobilised with the 25th (Cyclist) Battalion London Regiment upon the outbreak of the First World War and saw service as a Company Commander on the North-West Frontier of India. Closely associated with him in this work was his old friend Capt. Bruce Humfrey, J.P., Recorder of Croydon, and the late Lt.-Col. F. Harwood, M.C., J.P. Efficiently these three men set to work to restore order out of chaos, and laid a sure foundation for the organisation of the thousands of L.D.V's in the Zone area. Lt.-Col. Harwood assumed the duties of an Assistant Zone Commander, and in that capacity rendered magnificent service until his death on February 23rd, 1944. Capt. Bruce Humfrey organised the first and largest sub-Zone to be formed and afterwards became Zone Intelligence Officer. This sub-Zone was eventually organised into the 58th, 59th, and 60th Surrey Battalions, also Zone Headquarters, and included several hundred Purley men who formed "B" Company of the 58th.

In Coulsdon, Capt. R. G. Hudson—afterwards Major and second-in-Command of the Purley Battalion—undertook the formation of a sub-Zone to include men in Coulsdon, Purley (South of Godstone Road), Kenley, and Whyteleafe. Those who assisted him will always remember with gratitude the kindness of the late Mrs. Hudson, who, as a constant stream of men came to be enrolled.

often far into the night, supplied them with refreshment and acted as unofficial Adjutant while the organisation was in progress. When later on Battalions were formed this sub-Zone comprised "C" Company of the Purley Battalion.

The sub-Zone that eventually became "A" Company was organised from men in the Carshalton area, but upon the introduction of the Battalion system the latter was first known as "D" Company No. 3 Croydon Battalion, and it was not until the title of the Purley Battalion had been altered to the 58th Surrey, and the L.D.V. became the Home Guard, that it was transferred to the 58th as "A" Company of that unit.

Upon enrolment each volunteer was given an armlet, and if one of the lucky few he received a rifle and ten rounds of ammunition. Denim uniform of thin khaki material and field service caps which quickly followed gave the cartoonists full scope. The caps were the smallest ever; the uniform jackets had collars so large that it was said they were originally made for horses and passed out of service when the British Army was mechanised, but the L.D.V. took it all in good part and carried on.

Alterations to the uniforms were quickly effected; old soldiers proudly put up their medal ribbons, and it was not long before those who had jokingly referred to themselves as "Fred Karno's Army" began to move smartly to the word of command with the confident bearing of men under discipline.

All these men were volunteers; their country was in danger and they had come forward to defend it. They knew full well the sooner they could lick themselves into shape the greater their value as a fighting force. They lacked almost everything save courage and determination, so set about learning their job undeterred by ridicule or lack of arms, but proud in the knowledge that they were the "WE" of Mr. Churchill's defiant speech, "We shall fight on the beaches . . .we shall fight in the fields and in the streets". To them, as to all other stout-hearted Britons, these brave words were an incentive and inspiration.

The Nazi reaction to the formation of the L.D.V. was immediate and scathing. At first their radio stations jeered at them and asked what they were going to fight with when invaded. This was a problem which was puzzling the L.D.V., but when the Nazis afterwards announced they would shoot as *franctireurs* any they captured, this bucked them up tremendously and added considerably to their morale.

CHAPTER TWO

Commanders are Appointed

WHILE THE ORGANISATION of "Z" Zone by the late Major Gillett was in progress, its military command was placed in the hands of the late Major-General Nelson Anderson, C.B., C.M.G., D.S.O., a retired Officer with a distinguished military record. In the first world war he was eight times mentioned in dispatches, and in addition to his British decorations held the Legion of Honour and the Order of the Crown of Roumania. He was A.D.C. to His Majesty King George V in 1921. It is not too much to state that until his retirement under the age limit in May, 1942, he was the guide and friend of every L.D.V. in his area.

In 1920 he had been an instructor at the Staff College, Camberley, where among the students was an Officer who afterwards became his chief assistant at Zone Headquarters, the late Lt.-General Sir Douglas Brownrigg, K.C.B., D.S.O. The latter held the appointment of Adjutant General to the Forces in France until their evacuation, and upon his return to England was posted to the L.D.V. at Croydon, where he soon became a familiar figure. His lectures upon the tactics so recently employed by the German army were of inestimable value to a force like the L.D.V. where enthusiasm was greater than military knowledge. A very experienced soldier, with a breezy personality which appealed to all ranks, he served under Major-General Anderson all through the period that afterwards became known as the "Battle of Britain", and it was with great regret that the Officers and men of "Z" Zone said goodbye to him in February, 1941, when he was appointed to the command of "R" Zone.

Major-General Anderson had an unerring instinct for selecting the right man for the job, and his choice for the command of the Purley Battalion, or as it was then termed, No. 1 Battalion "Z" Zone, was Capt. R. L. Haine, V.C., M.C., Honourable Artillery Company and Indian Army. No better selection could have been made. From the day he took over command "Bill" Haine's ambition was to make his Battalion an efficient and happy one. In both he was eminently successful. A fine soldier, he set a high

["Croydon Times" Photograph.

MAJOR-GENERAL N. G. ANDERSON, C.B., C.M.G., D.S.O.

standard and insisted upon it being maintained. Under his leadership the Battalion worked hard to make itself a first-class fighting unit, and it can be truly said that none was happier in its work or had greater *esprit-de-corps*. Nothing was too much trouble for him to do for his Battalion. On parade he was a hundred per cent. soldier; off parade a very modest and unassuming man. He never ceased to impress upon Officers and N.C.O's that the efficiency and well-being of their men was a primary duty. Good men, he used to say, must have good leadership, and he thought his men deserving of the best. He insisted that every minute of training time was usefully employed, and woe betide any subordinate Commander who did not comply with this order. He was immensely popular with all ranks, and every Officer and man proud to serve under him.

From the beginning this newly-formed force had a genius for improvisation. At that time the Regular Army could give little or no help, consequently instructors had to be found from the men themselves. Rifles were available for perhaps one man in ten, so training had to be organised to make the best possible use of both instructors and weapons. There were no drill halls available in the locality in the summer of 1940, but many open spaces, and every evening these were thronged with men, some doing squad drill without arms, others being taught musketry by a former Army Officer or N.C.O., and usually one squad proudly drilling with the precious rifles. After a period of recruit drill, each squad in turn used the rifles until everyone received some elementary training with them. It was difficult to give instruction to a large body of men under these conditions, but there was such enthusiasm and goodwill that much was accomplished in a short time.

The speedy training of the individual was not the only matter of urgency. Defence posts had to be sited and constructed, slit trenches dug, obstacles prepared for blocking roads. Here was something everyone could do in defence of his home, and enthusiastically the work proceeded. Men fetched and carried, dug or filled sandbags, undeterred by blistered hands or aching backs. During the day members of the Battalion were at their civilian work in shops, factories and offices, but evenings and week-ends were times of feverish military activity.

The prelude to the "Battle of Britain" was on, and the first bombs in "Z" Zone, which fell on June 18th at Addington, not far from the Battalion area, were a sharp reminder that trenches and defence posts must be finished at all speed. In August large formations of enemy bombers attacked fighter aerodromes in the South and South-East of England, including Croydon and Kenley within the Battalion area, for the defence of which the 58th was responsible. There was always a chance that a bombing attack might precede a dropping of enemy parachute troops, and whenever a raid began every L.D.V. went immediately to his action station. On that memorable Sunday, August 18th, when the heaviest raid upon any part of England up to that time was made upon the Croydon, Kenley and Biggin Hill aerodromes, Platoon Commander William Battle, an old soldier who, in the first world war, had rescued his wounded Company Commander under heavy fire, rushed to his post and was instantly killed. It fell to this man to be the first L.D.V. to give his life for his country. From the beginning he had thrown himself into the work of organising and training his Platoon, and his untimely death was a great loss, deeply regretted by all who knew him. He was laid to rest in the presence of many of his comrades, his body being borne to the grave by Officers of the Battalion.

In September, 1940, the Local Defence Volunteers became the Home Guard, and the Purley Battalion received authority to wear the badge of the Queen's Royal Regiment (West Surrey), the famous Second Regiment of Foot whose battle honours cover almost every part of the world and in which many members of the Battalion served in the first world war. This was an honour greatly appreciated, and one which the Battalion throughout its service did its best to live up to.

At that time Battalion Headquarters was established in a small house in Whytecliffe Road, Purley, where Lt.-Col. Cuthbertson, formerly of the Devonshire Regiment, acted as Administrative assistant and Quartermaster. The men were still wearing denim uniforms but their L.D.V. armlets had been exchanged for those bearing the title "Home Guard". Only a few were in possession of rifles and ammunition, but every night their defence posts were manned, for the danger was then very real and close at hand.

The end of the Battle of Britain in October brought a feeling of relief, as no attempt at invasion had been made and it was realised the enemy had lost his finest opportunity. There was, of course, a chance, although a slender one, that an attempt might be made during the winter months and no precautions were relaxed, but it offered a respite which the newly-formed force could use for its organisation and training. A comprehensive syllabus of training was embarked upon; new tactics and new weapons had to be studied; everyone worked with a will to ensure greater efficiency in readiness for anything the spring of the following year might bring forth.

Weapon-training classes had no lack of pupils; every Company and Platoon worked hard to improve slit trenches and defence posts;

everything that effort and ingenuity could do in that direction was done. Arrangements for rapid calling-out of members in an emergency were overhauled and frequent tests made. It was realised the enemy had given us an opportunity of increasing our preparedness and we must take full advantage of it. Training had to be done under difficulties, but difficulties existed only to be overcome. Time for once was on our side; the evening training hours were too precious for any to be lost. Training continued while enemy bombers roared overhead; men dispersed only when bombs began to fall, and resumed their work when the "all clear" sounded.

All through the winter of 1940 men of the Battalion occupied each night the trenches they had dug on the bleak hillsides. However bad the weather, they were at their posts. Memories are short regarding the early troubles and trials of the L.D.V. It is one of the peculiarities of the British temperament that the old days are always the "good" old days, never the bad, and members are apt to forget that winter and the nights spent in the open in denim uniforms and without overcoats; when only the lucky ones had an issue of boots, and few heads could be found sufficiently small to fit the tiny field service caps. Steel helmets were then a dream of the future; but how anxious was everyone to be issued with them!

In his interesting book of memories, *Unexpected*, published just before Germany's defeat, the late Lt.-Gen. Sir Douglas Brownrigg, describing his early experiences with "Z" Zone, mentions that he visited many posts in the area at night and usually had a request for steel helmets, which inclined him to think the L.D.V. was in danger of becoming "tin-hat-minded" in the way the French had become "Maginot-minded". It is only fair to these men to present their point of view. They were doing duty in one of the most heavily bombed areas of the country at a time when the blitz was at its height. They were expected to leave their homes when more often than not the bombs were falling and their families had taken shelter. As the last civilian force to be formed, they realised they had to wait their turn for steel helmets, but found it difficult to reconcile the statement by the military authorities that none was then available when plenty were on sale in the shops and those who felt so inclined could purchase them. In fact, one enthusiastic commander who afterwards rose to high rank in "Z" Zone actually bought three hundred for his men, and had such a way with him that he eventually persuaded the authorities to pay the bill.

CHAPTER THREE

Reminiscences of 1940

IT IS DIFFICULT TO DESCRIBE the enthusiasm of the men who applied in their thousands to join the L.D.V.; they simply poured in, and like Barkis in *David Copperfield* were "ready and willing". One of the questions put to applicants was "Have you any knowledge of firearms?". The replies were often surprising. Those who had no such knowledge seldom admitted it for fear of being turned down, while others with considerable experience were so modest in their replies as to give the impression of almost complete ignorance. One applicant answered the question by stating that unless a naval gun was looked upon as a firearm he really had no experience at all. He proved to be a former Gunnery Instructor of the Royal Navy at Whale Island. Another individual, after diffidently admitting to having very little knowledge indeed of firearms, turned out to be a former big game hunter. But those to whom was assigned the duty of interviewing applicants were usually ex-Officers of the Army who could quickly sum up the suitability or otherwise of the person concerned.

Squad drill, which started almost immediately after enrolment, was not always performed strictly in accordance with up-to-date manuals of military training. It was several months before the latter became available, and in the meantime some of the instruction was reminiscent of *1066 and All That*. Still, enthusiasm was so great that in those first few months the force gradually became welded together and the groundwork of discipline laid. Men got to know each other and became used to working under a leader. At that time rumours of invasion were rife, the wildest stories were circulated—and swallowed; men were called out at all hours of the night, so often, in fact, that many preferred to sleep in their clothes. Barricades were thrown across the roads, and hapless motorists frightened out of their wits. Fearsome weapons made their appearance; mercifully there was no ammunition for them, otherwise our own ranks would have been depleted. However, as the weeks went by and subordinate Commanders underwent courses of instruction at military depôts and Zone Headquarters things

LOCAL DEFENCE VOLUNTEERS, 1940.

began to settle down. Training and discipline set its mark upon the men; shoulders were squared and figures which tended to droop with middle age became rejuvenated.

Future students of military history who read of the formation of the L.D.V. and its subsequent existence should remember it was never intended that either its organisation or training should follow "the precise routine of the Regular Army". Its original function was "to help to protect the country from the menace of paratroops", consequently there was an elasticity in training during the early months of its existence when invasion was a likely possibility. Guards and outpost duties were performed by squads of about ten men under a leader, all living in the same locality and knowing it intimately. These squads were trained to oppose any enemy landing in their area and prevent their getting away, also to report such information immediately and accurately by telephone or runner to their Headquarters. Communication was at first carried out by cyclist runners, afterwards by field telephone lines. These duties called for a system of training rather different from normal methods. Men were taught to be good shots and conserve their slender store of ammunition; to be expert in the use of ground and cover; to OBSERVE, REPORT AND OBSTRUCT. Their function did not call either for "spit and polish" or barrack square precision, but for a discipline and initiative all its own, which from the first the men were quick to acquire.

Later on, when the immediate danger of invasion passed and the authorities saw the potentialities of the force as a Home Defence army, also when it was seen how quickly the men responded to training and the use of automatic weapons, instruction proceeded on less "partisan" lines, but in the earliest days it may have been possible that a high-ranking regular Officer, when inspecting the men under training, had an uneasy feeling that "the Army was going to the dogs".

Whether class distinction existed in other units of the L.D.V. the writer does not know; certainly there was none in the 58th Surrey. It mattered nothing whether a man was a jobbing gardener or a jobbing banker; he was either a good soldier and a good comrade, or he wasn't; that was the only test. A leader was appointed because he had the qualities of a leader, not on account of his social position. At the same time there were many who would have made first-class leaders but could not give the necessary time on account of their exacting civil employment.

A wonderful spirit of comradeship speedily developed, and it was not long before the Battalion had an *esprit-de-corps* of its own. At first, old soldiers would proudly tell their comrades "I served with the old so-and-so's", but as time went on, "I am in the 58th" was said just as proudly, and friendly rivalry existed between Platoons and Companies, all anxious to excel for the credit of the Battalion. To help one another was the rule rather than the exception, and friendships were made between men in different walks of life which will continue in years to come.

A considerable amount of musketry training was done during the autumn and winter of 1940, and visits to Bisley were frequent, members usually travelling to the ranges by motor coach on Sunday mornings. These visits were highlights in our training and will long be remembered. There was always a welcome at the hut of the City Rifle Club, where it was possible to get a meal or the form of liquid refreshment which appealed to the palate of the individual.

Another outstanding feature of 1940 was the inclusion in our training of lectures by men who had served with the Spanish Republican Army. By them we were instructed in unorthodox methods of attacking an invader; how to creep silently towards him and end his existence with a cheesewire. Those of us who thought the sole purpose of the latter was for cutting cheese were speedily disillusioned, and the possible use of this somewhat unusual weapon of warfare was most enthusiastically received by many mild-eyed fathers of families, who for some months afterwards found a place for a cheesewire among their equipment on their nightly guards and patrols in the hope of practising their art upon some unfortunate Hun.

A School of Guerilla Warfare was opened at Osterley Park, which many members attended, becoming apt pupils. There they were taught camouflage, stalking and sniping, methods of using explosives to blow up railway tracks and ammunition dumps. Upon their return they lectured to their Platoons and Companies, and how eager their comrades were to learn!

The ranks of the Battalion included, as has already been mentioned, all sorts and conditions of men. We even had poets of no mean ability. The poem on the facing page was written by Pte. N. J. Fishlock in 1941.

One Year Ago

One year ago—eternity it seems!—
When wags were calling it the Bore War
When eggs and jam and onions weren't just dreams;
When headlines screamed if Heinkels neared our shore!

One year ago, the old sweats wondered how
And when and where this latest job would end;
For then, it seemed, the pace was deadly slow,
The road, monotonous, would never bend.

One year ago, a road called Higher Drive
Was just a dimly-known locality,
Where Purley's Upper Ten were thought to thrive,
And from their height look down on you and me!

One year ago, *that hut had never known
The thump of 'hipe', the reek of paraffin;
Its walls had never shuddered at the tone
And warmth of sundry yarns now told therein!

One year ago, "Blitzkreig" was but a word
Appreciated by the learned few;
Yet now, when near or distant crumps are heard,
The guard can still admire the moonlit view!

We most of us remembered Lewis guns,
But few had known of racks and pawls and sears;
Too many, then, forgot that Huns were Huns,
And had not changed through all the changing years.

One year ago, we fondly thought cheesewires
Were neat devices used for cutting cheese!
And Osterley, and Captain Crisp, and fires
In ammo. dumps—we had no thought of these.

The chap three doors from me, a year ago,
Was just—a chap to whom I said "Good-day."
What sort of man he was, I didn't know;
We Englishmen, I suppose, are built that way.

This comradeship, as yet, we did not know,
The shared anxiety, the shared relief;
We all were poorer then, a year ago,
For, gentlemen, we had not met—our Chief!

One year ago—and yet the balance shows
Our loss so little, and our gains immense;
When tyranny has melted like the snows,
These friendships, born of war, will live—years hence!

* on Higher Drive Recreation Ground.

CHAPTER FOUR

The Nightly Duties

GUARDS AND OUTPOSTS entered largely into the scheme of things throughout the existence of the Home Guard. Vulnerable Points (V.P's), Observation Posts (O.P's), and the various Headquarters, had their nightly quota of men on duty. At first, when the invasion scare was at its height, many points throughout the Battalion area were manned, but as time went on nightly duties were reduced to a security minimum. We were fortunate in having, both at Battalion and Zone H.Q., Commanders of great experience and human understanding. They knew these duties were done mostly by tired men, who, after they had finished them, went home for a wash and breakfast before beginning another day's work. Consequently many guards were subsequently either abolished or the number of men involved reduced; only the V.P's were heavily manned.

These duties were not always lacking in incident, humorous or otherwise. The following account of an early guard mounting by "A" Company is typical of the period, and may recall to one-time Section Commanders their apprehensions under similar circumstances.

The First Guard Duty
by "C"

Among the many interesting events that marked the service of the average Home Guard, none perhaps has left a more vivid memory than the first guard he performed. Inevitably the circumstances differed in each unit, but all shared alike the thrill of assuming active duty for the first time when enemy invasion was expected at any hour and, presumably, the anxieties attending the event.

This was certainly the case in No. 1 Section of No. 15 Platoon of "D" (Carshalton) Company, later to become No. 3 Platoon "A" Company of the 58th, when on June 20th, 1940, it was announced that a guard would be mounted as from Sunday, June 23rd, in Stanley Park Recreation Ground from 2100 to 0600 hours each day.

Typical of the unorthodox but efficient L.D.V. organisation, the Platoon was divided into six Sections in numerical order following the alphabetical sequence of the Section Commanders' names; thus the honour of commanding No. 1 Section, and the subsequent embarrassment of mounting the first guard fell to one "C". The latter aged visibly during the three days prior to the event, for he was beset with problems. He was an ex-Royal Engineer who had not mounted a guard since his pre-last-war Territorial days. He knew nothing of the qualities or military experience of his seven men; no specific duties had been laid down for his guidance and, to complete his discomfiture, he heard the O/C Platoon invite all interested Volunteers to turn out to see the first guard mounted.

By way of compensation, however, "C" was fortified by the knowledge that his guard would at least compare favourably with any local L.D.V. unit in the matter of arms, for the Platoon had acquired one .303 single-loading Martini rifle (minus foresight) dated 1895, one long Lee-Enfield (converted for .22) dated 1909, and one last-war S.M.L.E. rifle complete with bayonet, scabbard, pullthrough and oil bottle. This last weapon was for long to be the pride of the Platoon and, together with the unofficial ammunition—twelve rounds of .303 and twenty rounds of .22, was tenderly handed over by each Section Commander to his successor on guard.

To return to "C". That much worried man, after consulting his Second-in-Command Platoon as to the beat to be covered, spent many hours preparing a scale plan of the scene of operations, working out troop movements as applied to new and old guards, inventing orders which, if not to be found in any training manual, had at least a martial sound and, finally, in visiting the site to remove any stones which, by impeding the unaccustomed steps of the sentries, might lead to disaster.

At 2030 hours on the fateful Sunday evening "C", fully dressed in his L.D.V. armlet "uniform", his pockets bulging with all a fond wife thought essential for his sustenance during the night, and with three rifles and a bayonet tucked under his arms, set out for the Pavilion Guard Room. Possibly because he looked so much like a lost explorer he quickly gathered a retinue of interested juveniles, which ultimately became the nucleus of what appeared to him to be one of the largest crowds ever assembled in Carshalton. The O/C's invitation to all interested Volunteers to witness the spectacle had undoubtedly met with a generous response, for not only were all members of the Platoon present, but each seemed to have brought his wife, children and all available relations to see the fun.

In the secrecy of the Pavilion, "C" feverishly explained the plan of action to his Section, found two stout-hearted volunteers to act as the first sentries, and rehearsed the movements for "inspection", "slope" and "order" arms. At 2055 hours "C" marched out of the Pavilion with the S.M.L.E. rifle at the slope, turned about and proceeded to mount the guard in a manner undreamed of by any military body.

The result was surely a triumph of the adaptability and ingrained discipline of the British old soldier, for, despite the truly comic orders, lack of arms and uniforms, and the nerve-racking publicity, the guard carried things through with a slickness that was wholly admirable. Thus, with the sentries duly inspected, officially instructed in their duties, and each with a rifle at the "slope" marching solemnly outwards to the end of his beat, began the first of many guards conscientiously performed.

With the acquisition of proper arms, ammunition and uniforms, and the advantages of modern drill and organisation, subsequent guards gained much in military appearance, but the eager spirit and loyal support of those first few men, typical of many thousands of the L.D.V. and H.G., has never been surpassed.

A somewhat different experience fell to the lot of "B" Company's guard at Battalion Headquarters in Foxley Lane, Purley, on the night of December 8th, 1940. Section Commander H. N. Phillips, No. 6 Platoon, and Volunteers G. S. Bevington, L. M. Boor, and J. S. Stevens, of No. 8 Platoon, were on duty and had listened apprehensively to the wail of the siren.

Just before midnight a heavy raid began, and a high explosive bomb burst within twenty yards of the Headquarters, blowing in the front door and covering the occupants with splintered glass and *débris*. As they emerged from the building a rain water guttering crashed down narrowly missing them. They found a considerable number of incendiary bombs blazing around the Headquarters which they extinguished with earth and gravel scraped up by their steel helmets. They were then able to reach the ammunition store, by the blown-in entrance of which another incendiary was blazing furiously. Without hesitation they extinguished it and cleared away the *débris*, then, while the enemy bombers roared overhead, they removed the ammunition to a place of safety. When this was done, and the other incendiaries had been dealt with, the Section Commander reported by telephone to the Battalion Commander and Zone Headquarters. He and his men then collaborated with the police and A.R.P. wardens in dealing with several fires which had broken out nearby. In his subsequent report he expressed satisfaction with the conduct of his men under what he described as "trying circumstances". One cannot but agree that the circumstances *were* somewhat trying.

CHAPTER FIVE

The Battalion Takes Shape

IN SPITE OF MANY ALARMS, frequent guards and outpost duties, the shortage of modern weapons and qualified instructors, training proceeded steadily throughout the first winter and by the spring of 1941 the Battalion began to take shape. In March its title was changed to the 58th Surrey (Purley) Battalion and "HOME GUARD" flashes issued in place of the armlet. About that time "A" Company (Carshalton) was incorporated into it, and "C" Company, hitherto of double-Company size, divided into "C" and "D" Companies, the latter consisting of members resident in the Reedham, Purley (South of Godstone Road), Kenley, and Whyteleafe districts.

In February of that year the King's Commission was granted to Home Guard Officers, who received the appropriate ranks of their appointment. The Battalion Commander became a Lieut-Colonel, the Second-in-Command, also Company Commanders, were gazetted Majors. Seconds-in-Command of Companies became Captains, Platoon Commanders Lieutenants, and Platoon Officers Second Lieutenants. The appointment of an Officer was also authorised for the full-time duties of Adjutant and Quartermaster, and Capt. F. C. Crosse selected.

Later on Headquarters Company was formed, which completed the organisation of the Battalion on a Company basis as follows:—

Officer Commanding—Lt.-Col. R. L. HAINE, V.C., M.C.
Second-in-Command—Major R. G. HUDSON.
O/C Headquarters Company—Major H. C. BREWER.
O/C "A" Company—Major D. L. WAGHORN, M.C., D.C.M.
O/C "B" Company—Major A. J. CHAPMAN.
O/C "C" Company—Major L. PLOWMAN.
O/C "D" Company—Major W. C. DODKINS.

All had served as Officers in the First World War.

Of the original Company Commanders those of "C", "D", and Headquarters Companies remained during the existence of the Battalion. The command of "A" Company passed to Major A. L. Pash, M.C., in August, 1942, when Major Waghorn received an appointment in the Regular Army, and Major L. W. Ward was promoted to the command of "B" Company when Major Chapman became Assistant Commander "Z" Sector after the death of Lt.-Col. F. Harwood, M.C. in February, 1944.

It was during this period that one of the earliest volunteers, A. W. Harrison, D.C.M., M.M., bringing with him the wide experience gained in some twenty-eight years' service in the Regular Army, was appointed Regimental Quartermaster-Sergeant, and promoted Warrant Officer Class II; his ability and good service to the Battalion fully justifying this appointment.

In many ways the Battalion was more fortunate than some, not the least being the type of country from which it was recruited. A popular residential district in the extreme South of the Metropolitan Police area, it was bounded on its Northern extremity by the built-up locality of Purley, to the South by the broad expanse of Farthing Down, to the East by the village of Whyteleafe which lies in the Caterham Valley, and to the West by the picturesque village of Carshalton.

Within its boundaries was found almost every type of country; the rolling chalk downs with their open spaces; the valleys with main roads from London to the South Coast; woodland in profusion, villages and larger residential localities. It was very suitable for military manoeuvres and tactical schemes. If it lacked anything, it was congested townships for instruction in street fighting. But certain blitzed districts in South London were taken over by the military authorities at which specialised courses in this subject were held. The aerodromes at Croydon and Kenley within its area were a feature of frequent tactical exercises. Platoons worked over their Company areas; in Battalion schemes Companies operated over the whole area of the 58th, so that everyone knew the ground on which he might have to fight, and continually practised over it by night as well as by day.

Those well acquainted with the countryside in this part of Surrey grew to look upon it with different eyes now that we were at war. Woodland provided cover where men could be trained to move unseen. A spinney became of interest, not for its natural beauty or the primroses and bluebells found in profusion in springtime, but for its possibilities as a machine-gun post; open spaces because an enemy might descend and slit trenches must be sited to cover them; a field of buttercups gave opportunities for a field of fire.

On the roads it was the same. Certain spots held an attraction, not on account of the view but because they were suitable for anti-tank barriers to hold up an enemy advance towards London, while from cunningly sited and camouflaged trenches nearby the defenders could bring their weapons to bear upon the invader.

[*By courtesy of Tunbridge Ltd.*

COLONEL AMBROSE KEEVIL, C.B.E., M.C., D.L.

facing page 16

Liaison with the neighbouring Home Guard units was constantly maintained; they knew our dispositions to defend or attack, we knew theirs. From time to time Regular Army units were quartered in the area, and with them also the closest contact made. Everything possible was done to ensure that an enemy landing in any particular area would be confined to that area and liquidated.

Under the direction of the Zone Medical Officer considerable progress was also made with the training of First Aid personnel and stretcher bearers. The absorption of so many doctors into the Regular Forces left comparatively few in civil practice and these had many calls upon their services. But they were always ready to help the Home Guard and the Battalion owes a debt of gratitude to its Medical Officer, Major Leslie Meakin, and his colleagues who acted as Company M.O's.

In view of the possible damage to sewers and drainage systems, and the contamination of water supplies by bombardment or air raids, it was considered advisable that Home Guards should be inoculated, and considerable numbers of Officers and other ranks took advantage of this protection.

At all Battalion and Company exercises First Aid Posts were established as part of the operations, and casualties detailed with labels denoting their injury. Arrangements were also made for their speedy evacuation from Collecting Posts to the nearest civil hospital.

The year 1941 was marked by the award, in H.M. The King's Birthday Honours List, of the M.B.E. to the Battalion Weapon Training Officer, Capt. W. Fleming, an Officer of unbounded enthusiasm and energy, who, under the Commanding Officer's direction, supervised training on the most modern lines. Bristling with weapons and known as "Two-Gun Fleming" he was an outstanding figure on the rifle ranges, at the cinema shows of training films, and wherever else training was held under Battalion arrangements. He had ample scope for his abilities as the year went on, bringing rifles in good supply and many automatic weapons. When Capt. Fleming received an Army appointment his place was taken by another very capable Officer, Capt. A. L. Bryant, a splendid organiser. The 58th was always lucky in finding within its ranks "the man for the job".

Grenade practice and instruction in the handling of explosives were given a leading place in the training of the Home Guard. In this connection the Battalion was again fortunate. Major H. C. Brewer, in addition to Commanding Headquarters Company, gained a reputation for his work as Zone Bombing Officer. As an expert in the handling of grenades and explosives he was unrivalled. Cool as the proverbial cucumber, he inspired confidence in the hundreds of men he instructed. His frequent demonstrations were popular and widely attended; one could always be sure of "bigger and better bangs". This very capable Officer well deserved the Certificate for Good Service awarded him in January, 1944, and the M.B.E. in December of that year. His inseparable companions, upon the bombing ranges were Lt. H. S. F. Clutterbuck, M.M. and Sgt., afterwards 2/Lt. C. B. Povey. Together they formed a team which was instrumental in training all ranks of the Battalion in the handling and use of grenades.

Another outstanding figure was Capt. L. Weightman, appointed Battalion Intelligence Officer in June, 1941, and responsible for training a highly efficient Intelligence Section and Observers. The Battalion Defence schemes so ably prepared by him were models of information and detail. Liaison with Regular troops in the area and adjoining Home Guard units was another of Capt. Weightman's duties, which eventually exceeded the capacity of any one Officer to perform. Lt. W. M. Whiteman then took over Intelligence and Security, leaving Capt. Weightman free to devote the whole of his attention to the duty of Battalion Liaison Officer.

In October, 1941, the Battalion took part in the march of Civil Defence Services from Purley to Coulsdon Recreation Ground, held to inaugurate the district's War Savings' Week, and its smart and workmanlike appearance was widely commented upon. That same month "SY-58" titles were issued for wearing on the sleeves of battledress and greatcoat under the "HOME GUARD" flash.

Courses of instruction became available in increasing numbers and were widely attended. From the earliest days of the L.D.V. specialist instruction had been given at Zone Headquarters, also at London District and War Office schools and camps. The Commandant of the Guards' Depôt at Caterham gave every possible assistance in this connection, and short courses of training were given there to Officers and N.C.O's as far back as July, 1940. The 58th always acknowledged a deep sense of gratitude to the personnel of the Guards' Depôt for the assistance so readily given, and the Guards' training and discipline had a marked effect upon the Battalion.

Officers and N.C.O's who qualified as instructors at these courses had no lack of pupils when they returned to their Companies. Everyone was eager to learn the latest methods of warfare, and when a demonstration of every weapon issued to the Home Guard was given by trained teams in December, 1941, visiting experts expressed amazement that such a high standard had been

58TH SURREY HOME GUARD

reached by men who worked long hours at their civil occupations and could train only in the evenings and week-ends. Tactical exercises involving the manning of battle positions were held by Battalion, Zone and higher formations, in which Regular troops often took part.

An enormous amount of work was done that first year of the Home Guard's existence. Khaki serge battledress gradually replaced thin denim uniforms. Boots, leather belts, web equipment, steel helmets, and service respirators, were a general issue by the end of the summer, and most members had a greatcoat, the remainder being possessors of a voluminous cape. One cannot refer to them as "proud" possessors, as, although a very serviceable garment, for some reason or other it was never a popular issue, and its wearer an object of amusement to his comrades. However, it was not long before everyone had a greatcoat, and they were greatly appreciated.

By the end of the year the Battalion had been fully equipped and reached such a stage of efficiency that, had the necessity arisen, it could have taken a worthy place beside its comrades of the Regular Army. The spirit of service which prevailed was typified by the Commanding Officer's message to all ranks at Christmas, 1941—"We are a happy Battalion in which individuals are not working for their own ends but striving together in the team spirit for a great cause".

One cannot leave 1941 without mentioning the large number of members who had already gone from the Battalion into the Regular forces. Among them was Rodney Dove, who served in "B" Company from June, 1940, to December, 1941. His comrades little thought, when he left to join the Royal Navy, that he would achieve fame as one of the "human torpedoes" which sank an Italian cruiser at Palermo in January, 1943. Sub. Lt. Rodney Dove, R.N.V.R., was subsequently awarded the Distinguished Service Order for gallantry and devotion to duty, and although taken prisoner, used to write cheerful letters to his comrades in which he often referred with pride to the time he spent with the Battalion and the wonderful spirit of comradeship which existed there. It is with pleasure one can record that he was repatriated from a prisoner-of-war camp in Germany during the early part of 1945, and safely restored to his family and friends.

Such was the type of man who joined the Home Guard, and subsequently left it to perform still greater service to his country.

CHAPTER SIX

The Home Guard "Other Ranks"

WHO WERE THESE MEN who came forward to enrol in the L.D.V.? "Why didn't they go into the Services?" are questions sometimes asked. The answer is a simple one. They were men from all walks of life, some youngsters, some middle-aged. They were, in fact, those whom the Services did not require for a time, and some whom they did not want at all.

The area from which the Battalion drew its recruits was a suburban one. Many went to London each day, others were in business in the locality. It was a cross section of the British people and entirely typical of it; the artisan, the clerk and the tradesman. Some were directors of their firms, others employees; men of all classes and types, but whatever their station in life they met on common ground in the Home Guard.

The Warrant Officers and N.C.O's, Sgt. Majors, Quartermasters, Sergeants and Corporals were, more often than not, ex-sailors, soldiers or airmen of the First World War. Without exception in the 58th they were a fine type and spared no pains to learn the intricate business of modern soldiering. The Corporals were as proud of their rank as anyone, and although they did not take exception to the fact that Napoleon had once been a Corporal, they certainly took a poor view of Hitler having held a similar rank.

These W.O's and N.C.O's were the backbone of the 58th and to them was largely due the success of the Battalion. The majority gave the whole of their leisure to the Home Guard, were efficient and entirely dependable. Their Officers had complete confidence in them; in fact confidence in each other was the keynote of the 58th—you could always depend upon the other fellow.

Then behind the N.C.O's was that splendid body known as "private soldiers". The Home Guard was a peculiar force in many ways, as an Inspecting Officer discovered when he stopped before a man wearing a few ribbons and asked the usual question, "What did you serve with, my man?". "Oh!, I commanded the First

58TH SURREY HOME GUARD

Battalion of the Blankshires, Sir", was the reply, and the Inspecting Officer passed on definitely shaken. But although everyone had not been a Colonel, and there were quite a few who had not even been privates before they became members of the Home Guard, there were many ex-Officers in the ranks and a very considerable number of ex-N.C.O's. Together they formed the solid background that makes for a good Battalion, and their Officers were very proud of them.

The Home Guard was a great "supply-line" of man-power to the Services and many hundred members of the 58th were called up in their age groups. They found the training they had received in the Battalion of the greatest benefit. Leadership and discipline, combined in many cases with a high standard of proficiency in musketry and automatic weapons, brought speedy promotion. It was heartening to receive their appreciative letters and to welcome them at Headquarters when they came on leave.

CHAPTER SEVEN
From Defensive to Offensive

THE YEAR 1942 BEGAN WELL for the Battalion as January saw the award of the first Proficiency Badges in the Zone. Of the seven members who qualified no less than six belonged to the 58th. To acquire one of these coveted badges a man had to have proved himself a good shot on the ranges and to have thrown live grenades. He had to know all about his rifle and the various automatic and other weapons issued to the Home Guard. Map reading, first aid, the use of camouflage and cover, were other subjects in the syllabus, and every candidate underwent an extensive "general knowledge" test to show he was conversant with the names of all Officers in his Battalion, the positions of the various Headquarters, telephone boxes, police stations, railway stations, and all other information he might require to know in an emergency. The prize was a little diamond of red cloth on the sleeve of the battledress jacket. It was certainly the sign of a very efficient Home Guard.

In the New Year's Honours List the following were awarded Certificates for Good Service:—

C.Q.M.S. H. M. Johnson, M.B.E.	"D" Company.
Sgt. W. A. Cobb	"A" Company.
Sgt. J. Raindle	"C" Company.
Sgt. A. E. A. Ockenden	"B" Company.
Cpl. R. C. White	"C" Company.

Certificates of Merit were also awarded to Sgt. H. N. Phillips and Ptes. G. S. Bevington, L. M. Boor and J. S. Stevens for their work in removing live ammunition when Battalion Headquarters was hit by a bomb during an air raid.

From February 16th, 1942, service in the Home Guard was made compulsory but prior to that date members were allowed to resign. It was said by many this would be the end of the force and destroy its spirit. In point of fact it did neither; a mere handful of men resigned, mostly elderly members who felt the strain of continuous training, and an influx of recruits more than made good the wastage. Of this Battalion it can be said that compulsion rested lightly upon its members; they continued, for the most part, to attend parades with the same regularity as before, and no man with a reasonable excuse was ever penalised. The spirit of comradeship was so strong that men often attended parades when unfit, rather than their absence should let their Section down. No guard or other duty ever failed to be performed because of the absence of its members. The keynote of the 58th was always, "We trust you to do your best and know you will".

At a "Brains Trust" held by one of the Companies, a question asked was, "What does the Home Guard offer a man in return for much of his energy and leisure?" The answer given by a member of the Brains Trust, a private in the Home Guard, was this: "The Home Guard gives to its members the right and privilege of taking up arms in the defence of his country, his home and his loved ones. It teaches him how to use those arms to the best advantage, and by an intimate knowledge of the particular area he lives in, to defend it to the best of his ability. It teaches him discipline, loyalty to his superiors, and confidence in himself. Above all it offers him a comradeship unknown in civil life, in which men of different stations meet together and work together without thought of personal gain, but with the same object in view—the defence of their homeland". People have sometimes remarked "I do not know what you could see in the Home Guard". This is their answer!

The opportunities the Home Guard offered were not always limited to those within its ranks; one was certainly taken by "Q" branch of the Higher Command to dump upon us at the outset field service caps apparently made for pygmies and boots for a race of giants; the possible reasoning being, if they fitted nobody in the Regular army they were just what the Home Guard wanted. Old soldiers remembered those delicate touches of Army humour which included, in their days, the detailing of men to the cook-house who were useless on the parade ground. There could surely be no shadow of doubt that a man of whom the drill sergeants despaired would be quite conversant with the mysteries of cooking.

So for one reason or another the Home Guard had ample scope for indulging in that pastime so dear to the heart of the average Britisher—grousing. There was always something to grumble about, and although, with the gradual issue of proper uniforms, equipment, and weapons, most of our grievances disappeared, there remained from first to last the grouse about Socks, which the Government was adamant in its refusal to authorise despite many questions upon the subject asked in Parliament. Heavy marching boots wore out socks very quickly; men's own thin civilian ones lasted little time and were difficult and expensive to replace. However, there it was—quite a legitimate grumble, for although it was understood the French Foreign Legion were never issued with socks, they at least received a half-penny a day as pay, but the Home Guard had neither socks nor pay.

There was, it is true, a "subsistence" allowance of one shilling-and-sixpence for periods of duty in excess of four hours, and three shillings in excess of eight hours, but curiously enough this concession was not altogether popular in the Battalion, most members preferring to give their services for nothing, and when they received the allowance usually passed it over either to their "comforts" fund or the Battalion Benevolent Fund.

In May, 1942, shortly after the Home Guard celebrated its second birthday, Major General Anderson relinquished command of "Z" Zone to the very great regret of all its members. For two years he had been a familiar figure, and his old-world courtesy and charm endeared him to everyone. He had been in indifferent health for some time but never spared himself in the service of the Home Guard. When he died in July, 1945, every member of "Z" Zone felt his passing as a personal loss. In the true sense of the word he was an English gentleman. His successor was Col. Ambrose Keevil, M.B.E., M.C., who had been an Officer in "Z" Zone from the beginning and latterly Assistant Zone Commander. In the first world war Col. Keevil served with distinction in the Royal Munster Fusiliers and subsequently entered the Middle East Staff College. He was awarded the M.B.E. for distinguished services in the Balkans, the Military Cross for service in Palestine and a bar to the M.C. for gallantry in France. The French Government recognised his services by conferring upon him the Order of Merit. To the heavy responsibilities of his new task he brought considerable experience and dynamic energy. His efforts to promote the efficiency of "Z" Zone were no greater than his desire for the well-being of its members. There was not an Officer nor man of the Battalion who did not look upon him as a friend.

Capt. F. C. Crosse, the Adjutant and Quartermaster, retired early in 1942 under the age limit, and subsequently formed the local unit of Sea Cadets. Capt. Crosse, who was very popular with all members of the Battalion of which he was one of the original members, had previously been a Master Mariner, and during an adventurous career at sea, which began in the old sailing ship days, had risen to the command of the *Majestic* and *Berengaria*. To fill the vacancy caused by his resignation, Capt. R. E. Godfrey (Royal Artillery) was posted from the Regular Army as Quartermaster, and in August, 1942, Capt. H. C. Miller (Seaforth Highlanders) joined the Battalion as Adjutant. Both these Officers contributed in no small measure to the Battalion's success.

Apart from the transfer of Officers and Permanent Staff Instructors, the Regular Army continued to give valuable assistance by providing demonstrations of training and the attachment of Home Guard Officers to Regular formations. The effect of this was to raise the military efficiency of the force and keep it abreast of the latest methods of warfare.

An "all-night" exercise was held on August 29th/30th, 1942, during which members, in addition to manning their Battle positions, were fed under Service conditions, also, said some, "fed up" under Service conditions. The exercise was a strenuous one with frequent attacks during the night by a Regular "enemy". A Major of a Guards Battalion was attached to the Battalion as Umpire, and his report to the Chief Umpire read as follows: "I was more than satisfied with the efficient manner in which Officers and N.C.O's of the 58th Battalion carried out their duties. I could not wish for a better team".

No mention has yet been made of the fine spirit of co-operation which existed between the Battalion, the local Council, the National Fire Service and all branches of the Civil Defence. The Coulsdon & Purley Urban District Council had every reason to be proud of the efficiency of the whole of the full-time and voluntary services in their area and the efforts they made to foster it. Nothing was too much trouble for any of these bodies to do for the common cause. The Chief Warden, Mr. E. T. Burt, o.b.e., and his Deputy, Mr. Marsh, gave frequent lectures to members of the Battalion, so that everyone knew how "incidents" were dealt with and how best to help. Members were also trained in Light Rescue and other duties. During 1942 a number of the Wardens became members of the Battalion, and it can be said that no finer "recruits" ever joined its ranks.

In October, 1942, men began to be "directed" into the Home Guard by the Ministry of Labour and National Service. Many of these would have joined long before but were on Government work and subject to the Ministry of Labour's direction. With few exceptions they became worthy members of the Battalion and were a great acquisition to its strength. About this time the word "PURLEY" was dropped from the official title of the Battalion, which was henceforth known as the 58th SURREY BATTALION HOME GUARD.

Examinations for Proficiency Badges continued throughout the year, and a special message of congratulation was received by the 58th from the Zone Commander on being the first Battalion in the Zone to obtain one hundred of these coveted badges. In 1942, also, was formed the Battalion Mobile Reserve, mostly from younger men able to proceed at speed at any part of the area threatened by enemy attack. Another institution was the commencement of "Battle Drill", a combination of parade ground drill and tactical training evolved during the North Africa campaign. This was at first somewhat bewildering, but when the parade ground stage had been mastered and we came to its tactical application, the value of this revised method of training became apparent, for it was directed to the specialised instruction of each member of the combat unit in his own particular duty, so that by battlecraft, quick manœuvre, and fire power, the maximum offensive action could be produced.

By the end of 1942 the Battalion was completely organised as a fighting force, not only fully trained for defence, but well ahead with its training for the far more arduous duty of attacking the enemy. The rôle of the Home Guard had been changed from the Defensive to the Offensive, only possible by the high state of efficiency it had attained. It is divulging no military secret to mention that had the enemy landed, either by air or sea, he would have been allowed no rest or respite; the whole basis of training being directed to the task of exterminating him at speed.

CHAPTER EIGHT

Home Guard Weapons

THE RIFLES FIRST ISSUED to the Battalion, in a proportion of about one to each ten men, were of the Enfield 1914 pattern, calibre .303, and known as the "P.14". In the late summer of 1940 they were withdrawn for the use of the Field Armies then in course of formation, and a more generous issue made of a somewhat similar rifle from the U.S.A. of .300 calibre, officially described as the "P.17". These rifles were among the early deliveries to Britain of lease-lend war material generously given by the American Government, and were received by the Home Guard with feelings of relief and gratitude. To prevent any attempt to load them by mistake with the ordinary British Service ammunition, they were painted with a broad scarlet band, as also were all subsequent American weapons.

Before this redistribution, however, the Browning automatic rifle made its appearance. This also was of .300 calibre and similarly painted. Although clumsy in appearance, it was found, on the range, to be extremely accurate, either for single shots or bursts of fire and became a valuable addition to our equipment.

The issue of the P.17 was sufficient for nearly every member of a rifle squad to possess his own, and removed the grouse many old soldiers had at the outset when they found they were expected to share their rifle with others. Now a man could take his P.17 home and it was always to hand in the case of a sudden call-out. He could keep it clean and serviceable, become proficient with it on the ranges; it was his rifle and his responsibility. After minor adjustments had been made they proved very accurate weapons, and a high standard of shooting was obtained with them.

Obviously the rifle was the principal personal weapon, but while it was in such short supply some other means had to be devised to arm the remainder in an emergency. The home-made "Molotov cocktail" made its appearance—an empty beer, wine or spirit bottle filled with an inflammable mixture and ignited by a petrol-soaked rag attached to the neck. Had enemy armour appeared they would have been hurled upon them so that the blazing contents penetrated into the vents and set the tank on fire. This, at any rate, was what was *supposed* to happen.

These home-made grenades, the few issued rifles and a sprinkling of shot-guns and revolvers were the entire armament of the Battalion in its early days; there was barely sufficient ammunition to have fought much longer than a few desperate minutes. Months later the "Mills 36 grenade" was issued; this was an explosive grenade almost identical with the old familiar "Mills" of the previous war, and as such particularly welcomed by veterans of 1914-1918. Other types quickly followed; the "Sticky" bomb, designed to blast the tracks and armour plate of enemy tanks; the "Thermos", so-called because it was almost identical in shape to a vacuum flask; the "S.I.P." a self-igniting phosphorus bomb, and many others. Later, anti-tank mines were issued for the defence of road-blocks, but in the meantime Lewis Guns became available also the Vickers and Browning machine-guns. The Lewis and Brownings came from the U.S.A., from which source we also received the Thompson sub-machine gun, a short-range automatic weapon usually fired from the hip. These were the "Tommy" guns famous on the gangster films, but afterwards replaced by the "Sten", a mass-produced weapon which, in spite of its cheap appearance, proved its value as a personal weapon on the later battlefields of the war. It was issued to the Battalion in sufficient quantities to solve the armament problem for the rest of our embodied service.

No description of our weapons would be complete without mention of the famous Home Guard pike, which provided the newspapers and cartoonists with an opportunity for so many jokes and caricatures. For issuing these the Home Guard Directorate has been scoffed at and ridiculed, and, so far as the writer knows, has never sought to defend its action although there is a possible explanation. During the Russo-Finnish war it had been proved that a crowbar, thrust between the sprocket and track of a tank, was capable of stopping it. With this in mind, Home Guard units applied for crowbars, and, in due course, a number of heavy gauge steel tubes, about six feet long, were received, into one end of which had been spot-welded a long pattern infantry bayonet. It may be the authorities intended the heavy steel tube to be used as a crowbar, and added an obsolete bayonet to one end so that it could also be used as an offensive weapon, but from the first it was known as the Home Guard pike and greeted with derision.

Later in the war, the Battalion also had its quota of weapons classed as "sub-artillery". The Northover Projector was the first of these, in appearance a very "Heath Robinson" affair, but capable of firing both the Mills grenade and S.I.P. bomb with accuracy.

[*Photograph by E. F. Phillips.*

ON THE BISLEY RANGES.

facing page 28

This was followed by others considered important enough to warrant a place on the secret list for a time, the Spigot Mortar and Smith Gun. Then there was the "E.Y. rifle", an ordinary service rifle reinforced by wire so that a more powerful propellant could fire a Mills grenade from a cup-discharger.

For each new weapon issued, teams had to be trained, and no sooner were they trained than members were called up for service in the Forces and the process of training new teams was repeated. There was no lack of volunteers and trained teams were always ready. Enthusiasm never faltered; the possibility of invasion kept everyone at concert pitch. "It may happen to-night" was ever before the minds of both instructors and teams; had it happened, the Battalion could have been depended upon to make good use of its weapons.

There was subsequently still another exchange of rifles, American-made "Enfield 1914 pattern" of .303 calibre, taking the place of the P.17 which stood us in such good stead early on in the war.

CHAPTER NINE

Battle Inoculation and
Exercises with Regular Army

IN THE NEW YEAR'S HONOURS LIST, 1943, two other members of the Battalion were awarded Certificates for Good Service, viz :—

Sgt. R. A. Waine, M.M. . . . Headquarters Company.
Sgt. A. J. Harman, M.C. . . . "B" Company.

The first course in Battle Inoculation was arranged by Zone Headquarters in January, in which field training was demonstrated with live ammunition. For old soldiers it was no novelty to crawl into positions while machine gun bullets poured over their heads; they at least realised the necessity for keeping every part of their bodies close to the ground, but others on that occasion were of the ostrich type who, although careful to keep their heads down, were not quite so mindful of their hinder parts. Once their faults were pointed out, however, they were quick to correct them, and when the exercise was repeated the way they flattened themselves to the ground would have done credit to a worm.

During the same month a demonstration of Army Co-operation aircraft was given by the Royal Air Force, and members were able to see how quickly aircraft could arrive on the scene and deal with targets indicated to them by wireless. Members also fired a very comprehensive War Course with rifles and machine guns. The training of specialists in the use of camouflage, observation, signalling, etc. had reached a high level, and many signallers, when called up for service in the Regular Army, were accepted for the Royal Corps of Signals.

As from March 1st, 1943, the designation of "Z" Zone was changed to "Z" Sector, but this caused no change either in Command or organisation.

In April, 1943, the formation of Women Auxiliaries was authorised for service in the Home Guard as clerks and telephonists, drivers of motor vehicles and cooks. Many ladies enrolled under this scheme and did excellent work, releasing a number of men for more active duties. It cannot be said the Authorities were over generous to them in the way of equipment, as the only thing issued for their use and protection was a badge bearing the letters "H.G." Like the male members they received no pay; unlike the male members they were granted no subsistence allowance when on prolonged periods of duty, but were only too willing to give every possible help, and we remember their good service with gratitude.

To mark the occasion of the third birthday of the Home Guard a message from His Majesty the King was issued as a Special Army Order, and the Prime Minister broadcast to members on the evening of May 14th. Ceremonial Church parades were held throughout the Battalion on the following Sunday. A week later a detachment took part in the "Wings for Victory" parade, organised in connection with the Coulsdon and Purley Special War Savings Week. This was a parade of all "Services" and the smart appearance of the men from the 58th received favourable comment in the Press.

Spread over several miles of country, with many calls upon its members for nightly duties, it was not often the Battalion could enjoy the amenities of a week-end camp, but on Saturday, May 22nd, five hundred Officers and other ranks proceeded to Bisley by train and spent the night under canvas there. A comprehensive programme of weapon training on the various ranges was carried out, and as one report stated "the discipline and work were both in accordance with the high traditions of the 58th". This was the high spot of our training for 1943; as we marched from Bisley Camp to Brookwood Station on the return journey, every member of that column of disciplined men felt proud of the Battalion and all it had achieved in the three years of its existence. Much hard work had been done to make it fit to take its place, should it be called upon to do so, beside the Regular Army; many difficulties had been encountered and overcome, and in that month of May, 1943, we were confident that the Battalion, as a unit, was trained and ready to give a good account of itself in action.

The Training programme set by the Sector Commander for those summer months was more comprehensive than anything previously attempted. Whereas the previous winter had been devoted to "individual" training, the summer programme was entirely "collective". Tactical schemes, by night and day, were set for every Platoon and Company, always based upon the supposition of an enemy landing and the methods to be employed to deal with it. Battalion schemes followed and these culminated in various large-scale exercises in which Regular troops took part. All had code names and were mostly for a period of twenty-four hours during a week-end. Companies and Platoons fed their men from field kitchens, First Aid posts were manned, and every possible contingency provided for. Men were "called out" by the methods which had been constantly practised since the beginning, consequently they reported, fully armed and equipped, with twenty-four hours' rations, in a very short time after the summons reached them. By this time portable wireless sets were in general use, and enabled the Unit Commander to bring both men and weapons quickly to any threatened locality. After each exercise a conference was held and valuable lessons learned by all ranks. There was never any question of information being available only for a favoured few; everyone was in the picture, and as far as possible everyone knew all about it. There were occasions, on large-scale exercises with the "battle" occurring many miles away, when Companies and Platoons were short of information, but as a general rule every man knew what was happening and his own particular duty.

In June, an old friend of the Battalion, Chief Inspector McFarland, Metropolitan Police, was transferred from the district on promotion. From the earliest days he had given every possible help, also many excellent lectures on Police and Home Guard co-operation. In his farewell letter to the Commanding Officer he said, "I saw the birth of the 58th and watched its progress; I never made any secret of the fact that the Battalion stands 'second to none' and can assure you I am not alone in this opinion. The relations between the Home Guard and Police could hardly be bettered".

The appointment of C.S.M. L. C. Appleton to the rank of Regimental Sergeant Major was made in June. Sergeant Majors are not always popular, but R.S.M. Appleton was the exception, and although a strict disciplinarian was both liked and respected by all ranks. The Battalion was also fortunate in its Permanent Staff Instructors, Sgts. A. V. Goodsell, Royal Artillery; and W. Langridge, The Queen's Royal Regiment. Both were excellent instructors and rendered good service; they were always willing to help any Platoon. We were indeed fortunate to have two such excellent N.C.O's on the permanent staff.

Other events associated with 1943 were the introduction of wound stripes and service chevrons, also the beginning of a series of B.B.C. broadcasts to Home Guards which were of great interest to members. In September the Battalion took part in the "Anniversary of the Battle for Britain" parade and service at the Rotary Field, Purley, with various other contingents.

Towards the end of the year plans were made for the establishment of an Old Comrades' Association and Benevolent Fund, with representative members from each Platoon upon the Committee, so that it could begin to operate as soon as embodied service ended. Generous contributions were made by members in order that future cases of necessity could be assisted. The year closed with all ranks busily engaged upon the programme of training set by the Sector Commander for the winter months.

[*Photograph by E. F. Phillips.*

IN THE BOMBING BAY.

CHAPTER TEN

The Home Guard Officer

To MEET WITH ANY MEASURE OF SUCCESS the Home Guard Officer needed to be a "man of parts". It should be remembered that the powers conferred upon him by his appointment were those of Command but not of punishment, unlike his Regular Army equivalent in rank who has both, and a guard-room into which to lodge the defaulter. To produce an efficient Home Guard Unit it was necessary, first and foremost, to secure the men's goodwill and co-operation, as in the peace-time Territorial Army. Commanders with that experience found their task much easier.

To gain respect and confidence one had to be a good soldier who knew his job. He had to maintain his own authority and that of his junior Officers and N.C.O's. He had to be fair and just to all ranks. Above all he needed TACT—a very large ration of that indeed. A kind word of appreciation to the willing horse—how many there were of these splendid fellows—a straight talk to the few whose feet were apt to wander from the path of duty. He had to make every man who was pulling his weight feel he was his friend. He had to know every man's name—not an easy matter in a Home Guard Company where the numbers ran into hundreds. There were many who had some physical disability; others worked very long hours at their civil employment. These things had he also to know.

The problems of training, too, were vastly different from those of the Regular Army where men were more or less together in barracks, camps, or billets, where men paraded for instruction each morning fresh and rested; where all were medically fit for it. In comparison, the personnel of a Home Guard Company were spread over many miles of country. When they attended evening parades, or for guard duty, they had already done a day's work, and in many cases gone far afield to it under conditions of discomfort and strain due to blitzed communications. Some worked exceedingly long hours in shops, munition works and factories. These men were tired and could not be driven, but once their goodwill and co-operation was secured would give of their best—and did. There were many elderly men and others whose efforts were hampered by wounds of previous wars. These presented a problem of their own, as in order not to let their Company down they would work beyond the limits of their strength.

To hold the attention of such men instruction needed to be the best procurable. Each Company possessed efficient instructors; the Battalion Permanent Staff were always ready to visit Companies and Platoons; they had an excellent and appreciative audience as did the specialist Officers attached to Battalion Headquarters. Visits from the Battalion Commander were very popular, and during several winters he visited each Platoon in turn and, after an inspection of training, gave a friendly talk to the men. Sector Headquarters was always ready to help and some splendid lectures given by their staff. The Sector Commander, Col. Keevil, visited each Company in the Sector—fifty-one of them; a monumental task, but held his audience's closest attention for nearly two hours on each occasion.

Thus it will be seen that the Company or Platoon was not a unit entirely on its own; it was part of a large family, and the link which bound it was that of patriotism and service. It was a family to which we all felt very proud to belong.

What has been written as to desirable qualities of a Home Guard officer was equally true of the Warrant Officers and N.C.O's. Not to everyone were all the virtues given, but by doing one's best and striving always for the good of the common cause a happy and efficient unit was the reward.

Whatever grouses the Home Guard may have had in connection with weapons, equipment, or shortage of ammunition in its early days, there was one thing it was never short of, "paper"—known throughout the Army as "bumph". This was the most difficult thing the Home Guard Officer had to contend with, and literally the bane of his existence.

Never had any branch of the British Army so many rules for its guidance; never had any branch less time to contend with them. Printed papers, stencilled copies of typewritten instructions, often so badly reproduced as to be barely readable, poured into Battalion, Company, and Platoon Headquarters in an ever-increasing stream. Every man, every weapon, and every item of equipment, appeared to be dealt with by one regulation or another. We did our best to keep pace with them but found it well nigh impossible.

Battalion had a full-time Adjutant, Quartermaster, and a couple of clerks; it could have done with a Platoon of them. The only full-timer at Company Headquarters was one clerk, while Platoon Headquarters had none at all.

To the great credit of Sector, against which the full spate of paper was unleashed, every effort was made to stem the tide passing to Battalions, who made an equally brave effort on behalf of the Companies, and Companies on behalf of Platoons, but in the constant attempt to cope with it there was a tendency on the part of subordinate Commanders to become "chairborne" and to spend time in an Orderly Room which should have been devoted to supervising the training of their men.

This was deplored both by the Sector and Battalion Commanders, who knew only too well the difficulties Company and Platoon Commanders had to contend with in this direction. Constant instructions were issued to the latter that training must be given priority, but it was a headache for everyone concerned and usually resulted in their devoting to office work every evening that was not set aside for training.

Rightly or wrongly the Home Guard Officer sometimes felt that many in high authority did not appreciate the circumstances under which his soldiering had to be done; that each working day was occupied by his civil employment leaving only the evenings and week-ends available for military duties. He was willing enough to devote the whole of his spare time to the Home Guard providing it would make himself or his unit more efficient, but to spend so much of that time in the preparation of endless streams of returns added to nobody's efficiency and he could see no sense in it. As one writer has very aptly said, "it caused the red, white and blue of an Officer's enthusiasm to become very definitely browned off".

CHAPTER ELEVEN

The Boys of the 58th

ONE EVENING, in the early summer of 1941, an elderly man, wearing an ill-fitting denim uniform with a few faded medal ribbons, was talking to a group of lads, the "youngsters" of the Home Guard, who were waiting their call to the Services. These were the "runners" who, in the event of an enemy landing, would have borne the news from the outposts to Headquarters, typical care-free and cheerful boys of the type seen on school playing fields. They had spent an active hour at physical training and games; their happy laughter had rung out as they threw the medicine ball at each other. Now, resting, they were listening intently to stories of famous battles in history, in which a gallant part had been played by the Queen's Royal Regiment, whose badge they were proud to bear.

As the lecturer went on to tell of brave deeds done in bygone days, and how it was the duty of every Britisher to give of his best in the defence of his country, he looked at those eager young faces and his mind went back along the years. To the days when as a youngster like those in his audience, he saw himself listening to much the same story from an old soldier of a previous generation; he saw himself training in peace-time for the stern business of war. He remembered how he and his comrades of the Territorials were jeered at as "Saturday afternoon soldiers"; he remembered, too, when Germany plunged the world into the 1914-1918 conflict, how glad he was he had learned sufficient of the art of peace-time soldiering to appear on the roll of his unit as a "trained man".

Since then a whole generation had gone by; he was now middle-aged, while his audience were boys about to face the perils of active service overseas. Not for them frantic efforts to claim exemption from military service; not for them a conscientious objection to fighting but none to eating a full share of the food brought to these shores by the gallant men of the Merchant Navy. They were ready to face the dangers and privations of war, clear-eyed and undismayed. Looking at those boys and realising that every generation had produced others like them, he thought of the words of the song "There'll always be an England".

These lads played a worthy part in the war; some came unharmed through many adventures; some will bear upon their bodies the marks of wounds for the rest of their days. Some, alas, lie in a foreign land in a spot that will be for ever England, but their memory lives on and we shall never forget them.

These young Home Guards had their own messages in Company Orders. In January, 1942, appeared the following:—

A New Year Message to our Young Soldiers

To you is handed the torch of freedom! Hold it high and keep it burning for Britain's future is in your hands.

Your fathers won the last war! There is much you can learn from them—their courage, their endurance, their cheerfulness in adversity. It is no fault of theirs that the Hun has again destroyed the peace of the world, but it is up to all of us to see he doesn't do it again.

Work hard at your weapon training and become skilful in the use of arms. Be ready when the time comes and never lose heart.

> *Life's battles don't always go*
> *to the strongest or fastest man;*
> *But sooner or later the man who wins*
> *is the man who thinks he can.*

Let those who read these words spare a moment to think of the future of the boys who fought and survived the war. One of the earliest to leave this Battalion managed to get into the Regular Army by over-stating his age. He served in North Africa, was captured, and went as a prisoner-of-war to Italy. He escaped, joined the partisans and served with them until able to rejoin the Army during the Italian campaign. Then, demobilised and partially incapacitated by wounds, for a long time he tramped the streets of London looking for work.

Can we better repay the debt we owe to the flower of our youth, who gave their lives for our country, than by helping the survivors to become self-supporting in civil life? The Government does for them what it can, but is helpless without the co-operation of those who can give employment. They offered themselves without counting the cost; with no thought whatever of their own future. They fought to gain the victory and if they ask our help, let it never go down to history that we failed them.

CHAPTER TWELVE

1944-The Last Year of Embodied Service

THE NEW YEAR'S HONOURS LIST contained the names of six more members to whom Certificates of Good Service were awarded, viz:—

Major H. C. Brewer	Headquarters Company.
R.S.M. L. C. Appleton . . .	Headquarters Company.
Sgt. P. A. R. Huckwell . . .	"A"	Company.
Sgt. W. A. Crocker	"B"	Company.
Sgt. C. H. Ayling	"C"	Company.
Sgt. J. E. Hobbs	"D"	Company.

A Certificate of Merit was also awarded to Capt. R. E. Godfrey, R.A., the Quartermaster.

A feature of the early part of the year was the training of Junior Leaders under the Adjutant, and N.C.O's who attended these courses greatly benefited from the instruction. Lectures in leadership had always been given high priority in training. The Commanding Officer, in his talks to Officers, stressed its importance, as did Company Officers to their N.C.O's. Every effort was made to see that subordinate Commanders were capable both of instructing and leading their men; there was neither fear nor favour in the selection; one standard was set for Officers and N.C.O's alike, leadership and efficiency.

It was a custom of the Battalion to do as much "out-of-doors" training as possible. Whenever the weather permitted, every type of field work was practised again and again, by night and day, so that all ranks could be depended upon to deal with any emergency. The Commanding Officer continually impressed upon members that if trouble came it would come quickly and they must be ready to deal with it. To that end parade ground drill was kept to a minimum and maximum time devoted to training for battle.

One cannot look back upon the spring of 1944 without mentioning the sorrow felt by all ranks of the 58th at the death in February of Lt.-Col. Frank Harwood, M.C., Assistant Commander "Z" Sector. Although never a member of the Battalion he lived in its area and was widely known and respected. One of the faithful few who, in the early days of the L.D.V., were responsible for the organisation of "Z" Zone, from the first he devoted to it all his time and his very considerable ability. He was so modest and unassuming that not until one grew to know him was it realised what a brilliant brain lay behind his kindly smile, or how great his love for his country and his fellow man. For both he laboured beyond the limits of his strength, and left with all who knew him a memory that time will not dim.

The vacancy caused by his death was filled by the appointment of Major A. J. Chapman, O/C "B" Company of the 58th, as Assistant Commander "Z" Sector with the rank of Lieut.-Colonel. Sorry as the Battalion was to lose this popular Officer, it was felt no one could have been selected more capable of carrying on Lt.-Col. Harwood's work, and his appointment was an unqualified success.

It was well known, in those early months of 1944, that the "Second Front", which had long been the main topic of conversation, might be launched at any time, and training throughout the Battalion reached a high peak of effort. Our armies were trained and ready to invade. The Home Guard was ready for any duty it might be called upon to perform. Not as in May, 1940, when a few patriots armed with sporting guns watched the night skies for paratroops, but as trained Battle Platoons, heavily armed with modern automatic weapons and ammunition in plenty. Thus we stood in May, 1944, with our nightly Task Platoons on duty all over the country, and behind them perhaps fifty times as many men trained and ready.

In the months that had passed, men had attended courses in almost every branch of the military art; now, in readiness for whatever retaliation the enemy might make, hundreds of members were trained in Light Rescue work by the local Civil Defence personnel, and in First Aid by Company and Platoon instructors. There was a feeling of expectancy in the air; anything might happen and we must be ready. To mark the fourth anniversary of the Home Guard His Majesty the King issued the following "Order of the Day" :—

"The fourth anniversary of the Home Guard falls in a year when the duties assigned to you have a very special importance.

"To the tasks which lie ahead the Home Guard will be able to make a full contribution. I know that your greatly improved efficiency, armament and leadership render you fit in every way for the discharge of these tasks.

"The burden of training and duty, dependent as it is on the needs of war, cannot fail to fall with greater weight on some than on others. To that great number of you who combine proficiency and enthusiasm in Home Guard work with responsible work of national importance in civil life, I would send a special message of thanks and encouragement.

"To all of you I would like to express my appreciation of your past service and my confidence that you will continue to carry on in the same high spirit of patriotism that you have always shown, until the day of victory."

To mark the anniversary a detachment from a London Battalion of the Home Guard provided the guard at Buckingham Palace for a period of twenty-four hours.

The following message was also sent from "Z" Sector Commander to all ranks:—

"To-morrow we begin our fifth year of service.

"We have the honour in this vital hour to be responsible for the defence of a large and most important part of the capital of the British Empire.

"The tasks ahead of us may be unexpected or they may be difficult, but we have every confidence we shall be more than equal to every demand.

"Let each of us by our unselfish spirit and our disciplined bearing be an inspiration to all with whom we come in contact, remembering always that as Home Guards our duty is not only to defend our native land but to maintain its finest traditions."

Frequent "snap-tests" were held when Companies and Platoons engaged upon normal training duties were called out suddenly to deal with a certain tactical situation. Everyone was "on his toes" and ready for anything. Battle Platoons "stood to" every night ready to move immediately to a threatened area; communications were tested, weapons inspected, motor vehicles given a final check over; nothing left to chance. Then came "D" Day on June 6th, the great day to which everyone had looked forward for four long years. It came—and went, and once again British and Allied armies were fighting on French soil.

The news of the successful landings without any immediate retaliation upon this country came as an anti-climax; somehow or other it did not seem possible the Nazis would take it "lying-down". We waited, but waited in vain, for the long anticipated call-out, and nothing happened. A more serious look, perhaps, upon the faces of the men in the Task Platoons; a more frequent cleaning of rifles and automatic weapons; a careful inspection of each round of ammunition. Every man on those nightly duties knew that at any moment something *might* happen, but for several weeks nothing did. Then came the German reply—the V.1—the flying bomb, and the air-raid sirens blared continuously.

No less than 136 of these pilotless aircraft fell in the Battalion area and on its immediate borders, causing damage to nearly 26,000 houses. In the Urban District of Coulsdon and Purley alone, 10,489 houses had previously been damaged by bombs from piloted aircraft.

Possibly because most of the houses in the area were of a detached or semi-detached type, and there were few large blocks of residential flats, casualties were mercifully less than they would have been in a more congested locality. In the Urban District of Coulsdon and Purley ninety-two people lost their lives and 765 were injured as the result of air raids. During the flying bomb attacks twenty people were killed and 432 injured in Beddington and Wallington, while the neighbouring Urban District of Carshalton had twenty-five killed and 442 injured.

Under this indiscriminate bombing the spirit of the people never wavered; in fact, their courage was an inspiration. The story is told of one shattered house where an old lady of eighty-five lay bed-ridden. The ceiling of her room was open to the sky; the floor deep in *débris*, and plaster covered her bed. She had had a wonderful escape as with the exception of a few bruises she was unhurt. When it was suggested she should be moved to a neighbour's house she was most indignant and repeatedly told her would-be rescuers "I'm not going. I'm not afraid of Hitler!"

At this stage of the war people in the South of England had become accustomed to "carrying on" whatever the circumstances, and while the flying bombs screamed overhead the parade organised in connection with the "Salute the Soldier" Week was held and a full muster of the Battalion marched from Coulsdon to the Rotary Field, Purley, to be inspected by the late Lt.-General Sir E. C. A. Schreiber, c.b., d.s.o., General Officer Commanding South-Eastern Command, also providing the Guard of Honour. There were many bangs while the General passed slowly along our ranks as we stood stiffly to attention, and although he afterwards congratulated us upon our steadiness it is only fair to confess that many did not feel quite as steady as they looked.

For the remaining months of embodied service the Battalion performed a task never visualised as its only reply to German attacks upon this country—rendering assistance at flying bomb incidents, but this was carried out with the same enthusiasm as other duties. Arrangements were made for trained teams to be held in readiness every evening and during the weekends, and these reported immediately to the Civil Defence Incident Officer whenever assistance was required.

With the passage of time many things are forgotten, but few of the people who lived in "Z" Sector during the flying bomb period will ever forget it. Every public service gave of its best and was an example to the world of devotion to duty.

Magnificent work was done by our comrades of the Civil Defence, in which the Home Guard was proud to take part. Damaged houses were given first-aid repairs, roofs re-tiled, and broken windows covered. Few of the Home Guard had any previous experience of repairing houses but soon acquired some measure of skill. One remembers a particular "incident" when a member of the Battalion, a solicitor of repute in civil life, was seen perched upon the damaged roof of a house replacing tiles with the same precise attention to detail as had no doubt brought him to eminence in the legal profession. It was not uncommon for members of the Battalion to report when called upon to do repairs to the homes of others while their own were similarly damaged.

The Inspector General of Civil Defence, Ministry of Home Security, wrote to the Director General, Home Guard, as follows:—

> "Your Home Guard have been giving us magnificent help during the present troubles with the Flying Bomb, and I should like to express to you and all of them our very warmest possible thanks and gratitude for what they are doing."

Many other tributes to their work were received from Local Authorities and others whose homes had suffered from this type of bombing which the enemy mistakenly imagined would break the spirit of the people of Southern England.

On the evening of September 6th, 1944, Sir James Grigg, Minister of War, broadcast the decision of His Majesty's Government regarding the future of the Home Guard, and stated that as from September 11th all compulsory drills and training, including assistance to Civil Defence, would be discontinued and future duties performed on a voluntary basis. There was no lack of volunteers for the latter, and duties continued to be done until November 1st, from which date the Home Guard was ordered to "Stand down" but to remain embodied and ready for action in case of emergency.

Message to the Home Guard in "Z" Sector

Today you stand down from your operational and training duties after four-and-a-half years of active service.

You have built up a reputation second to none in the country by your fearless and devoted work week in and week out.

You have the proud satisfaction of knowing that your reputation has never stood higher than at the present time and that you have gained the complete confidence of the civil population and the Military Authorities.

The work of the Home Guard has been of the utmost value in the successful prosecution of the war and this will be realised more and more as time goes on.

Remember, however, that although we are standing down our work is not finished, we must be ready to fall in again should this be necessary and every one should join our local Home Guard Association, so that together we may carry on our great tradition of unselfish and willing service for the benefit of our neighbourhood and the men and women still serving in the armed forces and thus help to build a happier and a better England.

I wish to express my personal thanks for the loyal co-operation and the countless acts of kindness I have received from all ranks during these last few years—it has been an honour to command such men as the Home Guards of "Z" Sector.

May God bless and speed each one of you.

A. KEEVIL,
Colonel.
Commanding "Z" Sector H.G.

"Z" Sector H.Qs. H.G.
1st November, 1944.

Such is the story of the 58th Surrey Home Guard, of its four and a half years' existence, and the names of the few who took part. To record the name of everyone who contributed to the success of the Battalion is obviously impossible, suffice it to say they were equally deserving of mention. The 58th came into being at a time when Britain stood alone and the danger of invasion very real. Its members, ordinary residents of the neighbourhood, and the splendid women who worked as Auxiliaries, laboured, not for personal gain, but because they loved their country and wanted it to remain free. 'Tis said that had the enemy invaded in the summer of 1940, Britain would have been defeated; that is a matter of opinion. Had this come to pass, one thing, however, is certain—there would have been an "underground" movement the like of which the world has never seen. The members of the 58th offered themselves when their country called; over a thousand of their number passed into His Majesty's Forces, many of whom laid down their lives. They did all that was asked of them, and more. That they never came into action against the enemy is no fault of theirs—they were ready, but he would not risk it.

Thus came the end of the adventure. It is said the Home Guard numbered at "Stand Down" a million and three-quarters trained men; possibly three million passed through its ranks—three million who carry into that brave new world the comradeship and understanding of the other fellow's point of view they learned in the Home Guard.

On Sunday, November 26th, 1944, the Battalion took part in the Sector parade at the Davis Theatre, Croydon, when the late Rt. Hon. Brigadier Lord Croft, C.M.G., D.S.O., Under-Secretary of State for War, addressed the Home Guard of "Z" Sector. This was followed by a march past, and the Salute taken at Croydon Town Hall by Sir Malcolm Fraser, Bart., G.B.E., H.M., Lieutenant for Surrey.

The "Stand Down" parade was held at the Drill Hall, Marlpit Lane, Coulsdon, on Sunday, December 3rd, 1944. After a short drumhead service Lt.-Col. R. L. Haine, V.C., M.C. inspected his Battalion for the last time and gave a short address, which was followed by a march through Coulsdon and Purley, past the Council Offices in Brighton Road, from the steps of which he took the salute.

It was a dull and rainy day as we stood in Battle Order to hear the farewell message of our Commanding Officer; we had come to the end of the journey. It should have been a joyful occasion, as all danger of invasion had passed, and the enemy, so powerful when the L.D.V. came into existence, was being utterly defeated. Britain, in spite of all her sufferings, had escaped the fate of Europe. She had neither been fought over nor occupied; yet there was sadness in our hearts as we marched away to disperse by Companies, to think this was the last time we should appear together in uniform, bound by the ties of service, danger, and comradeship. The Home Guard had taken all we could give it, but how much more had it given us?

Message from His Majesty the King to the Home Guard

For more than four years you have borne a heavy burden. Most of you have been engaged for long hours in work necessary to the prosecution of the war or to maintaining the healthful life of the Nation; and you have given a great portion of the time which should have been your own to learning the skilled work of a soldier. By this patient, ungrudging effort you have built and maintained a force able to play an essential part in the defence of the threatened soil and liberty.

I have long wished to see you relieved of this burden; but it would have been a betrayal of all we owe to our fathers and our sons if any step had been taken which might have imperilled our Country's safety. Till very recently, a slackening of our defences might have encouraged the enemy to launch a desperate blow which could grievously have damaged us and weakened the power of our own assault. Now, at last, the splendid resolution and endurance of the Allied Armies have thrust back that danger from our coasts. At last I can say that you have fulfilled your charge.

The Home Guard has reached the end of its long tour of duty under arms. But I know that your devotion to our land, your comradeship, your power to work your hardest at the end of the longest day, will discover new outlets for patriotic service in time of peace.

History will say that your share in the greatest of all our struggles for freedom was a vitally important one. You have given your service without thought of reward. You have earned in full measure your Country's gratitude

(Signed) GEORGE R.I.
Colonel-in-Chief.

An extract from the last weekly Orders of "D" Company of the Battalion, afterwards reproduced in the March, 1945, issue of "DEFENCE", is given below:—

This, then, unless the unexpected happens, is the end; the end of the weekly messages your Company Commander included in Orders; the end of our soldiering together but not of our comradeship, which will continue in the Old Comrades' Associations.

You have been thanked for your services by His Majesty the King, by high military commanders, the civil authorities and the public, but in your heart you wanted no thanks at all; your greatest reward for what you have done was the still small voice of your conscience, and the knowledge that you had satisfied yourself.

So now, with the memory of our last parade fresh in our minds, and the thanks of the country ringing in our ears, we can look both to the past and the future. To the early days of the L.D.V., when we stood guard under the night skies with the sound of the guns at Dunkirk coming faintly to our ears; to the nights when the earth was torn asunder by bombs and we feared, not for ourselves, but for those we loved; to the times we have worked together and trained together, and in doing so found what a decent chap the other fellow was. To happy days at the ranges, and our pride when we scored a bull; to the cups of tea handed out with a smile by those splendid ladies of the W.V.S.; to the smell of wood smoke from the armourer's fire; to the night when old so-and-so, quieter than usual, told us his only son had died for his country, and how, in our rough way, we tried to console him, feeling if we succeeded, it was because of what we meant to say rather than what we said.

These things and many more shall we remember of the days and nights we trained for the battle never-to-be, and when we look back and think of the grand fellows we knew we shall say 'These were men'.

[*German official photograph by courtesy of Keystone Press Agency Ltd.*
As the Home Guard Stand Down Hitler's Volkssturm Stand To.

58TH SURREY HOME GUARD

What of the future? Although the days of our soldiering are over our opportunities for further service remain. It is still left to us to do something more to make this world a better place if we live up to our motto "Service not Self". A helping hand to our fighting men when they return, especially old comrades from this Battalion. An interest in the youth who will carry on when we are gone so that they grow up to serve the country and keep the flag flying as we have tried to do—what inestimable value to the Army Cadet Force the ability and experience of some of our members could be; AND a greater interest in local and national affairs so that only those capable and willing to work for the good of the community, only those who will see that Germany is never again allowed to start another world war—will be elected to represent us.

There is, indeed, much we can do if only we stand together; as individuals we can do nothing, but through their Old Comrades' Associations the million-and-three-quarter Home Guards could, if they wanted to, become a power in the land. Let us strive to make it so.

To end the story of the active life of this Battalion, in which 3,216 men enrolled between 1940 and 1944, no more fitting words can be used than those in the farewell message of General Sir Arthur Smith on relinquishing command of London District to take over the duties of General Officer Commanding-in-Chief, the Persia and Iraq Command:—

It is my earnest desire that the spirit of the Home Guard may always live, for this will be of the greatest benefit to our country in the future.

Subsequent to the "Stand Down" of the Home Guard, H.M. the King recognised the meritorious service of various members in "Z" Sector by conferring a number of awards. Among them were two of particular interest to the Battalion, viz.:—

"Z" Sector Commander, Col. Ambrose Keevil, M.B.E., M.C., promoted Commander of the Most Excellent Order of the British Empire.

58th Surrey Battalion, Major H. C. Brewer, appointed member of the same Order.

The following Certificates for Good Service were also awarded in the New Year's Honours List, 1945:—

R.Q.M.S. A. W. Harrison, D.C.M., M.M	Headquarters Company.
C.Q.M.S. F. C. McClelland, M.M.	"A" Company.
C.Q.M.S. F. A. Savage	"C" Company.
Sgt. H. J. Hartley	Headquarters Company.
Sgt. A. E. Cumings	Headquarters Company.
Sgt. S. J. Parker, M.C., D.C.M	"B" Company.
Sgt. J. H. Ware	"D" Company.

CHAPTER THIRTEEN

1945 - The Year of Victory

AFTER "STAND DOWN" there began for those connected with the administration of the 58th what can best be described as "The Great Clear-up". Weapons, stores and equipment called in, checked and returned to the proper authorities, certificates of service issued to members. Companies and Platoons closed their "Comforts" and similar funds and disposed of their private stores. Most headquarters closed down during the early months of 1945, and as requisitioned premises were vacated they were handed over to the Surrey Territorial Army and Air Force Association.

Battalion Headquarters was transferred for administrative purposes to Marlpit Barracks, where the Quartermaster continued to grapple with the many problems involved until everything was settled and he was reposted to his Regular Army unit at the end of June.

There was still a good deal of activity apart from the "official" side of the Battalion. Photographers were kept busy taking pictures of the different formations; rifle clubs, assisted by the Surrey T.A. and A.F. Association as regards rifles and ammunition, were formed and have since been well supported by members. Old Comrades' Associations began to function and many social events held; the Battalion Benevolent Fund has helped cases of distress; employment found for former members upon demobilisation from the Forces.

A number of Officers and other ranks joined the Army Cadet Force and are taking part in the training of our youth in citizenship, comradeship and discipline—qualities no less necessary to-day than during the war years. Many members joined other youth organisations.

No call was made upon the 58th during that fateful year of 1945, a year which saw the complete defeat and unconditional surrender of Germany, Italy and Japan, and terminated the "state of emergency" which brought the Local Defence Volunteers into being in May, 1940. Towards the end of the year it was announced the Home Guard would be disbanded as from December 31st.

So as the old year ended there passed into history that modern counterpart of the levies called to arms by King Alfred over a thousand years before to give battle to the invading Danes.

Units which manned the anti-aircraft guns were the only ones brought into action against the enemy. General Service Battalions, such as the 58th, stood trained and ready, but were never called upon to fight. We know now what we did not know as we watched the battles in the summer skies during the months of August to October, 1940, that had the gallant "few" of the Royal Air Force, who flew the Spitfires and Hurricanes, failed in their seemingly impossible task of destroying the Armadas of the Luftwaffe, invasion fleets would have sailed from the Continental ports as soon as the enemy had gained command of the air, and the Home Guard, with its few rifles, shotguns and pikes would have had to do its pitiful best against the armed might of the Hun.

It was a miracle that saved us then. Let us never forget that but for the bravery and skill of the fighter squadrons of the R.A.F., the horrors of Belsen might have been known in this fair land of ours.

Whether the plans of the enemy were affected by the mere existence of the Home Guard may never be known, but one thing cannot be denied—the presence of nearly two million part-time soldiers enabled the Higher Command to denude these islands of Regular troops and despatch them for service overseas. Nor can it be denied that the Home Guard performed many duties which would otherwise have had to be done by the Regular Army, and in consequence the training of the latter was able to continue uninterrupted.

None who ever served in the Home Guard will forget the wonderful spirit which animated all ranks, its cheerfulness, comradeship, or voluntary service to the community. It was but one of many voluntary services that war brought into being; each and all deservedly proud of their record. If the spirit which animated them prevailed throughout the world to-day, the spirit of "Service not Self", many problems which now beset us could either be remedied or solved. Without this spirit the world will be far removed from the lasting peace which so many have given their lives to secure.

In February, 1946, the death was announced of Lt.-General Sir Douglas Brownrigg, K.C.B., D.S.O., only a few weeks after his lecture to the Home Guard of "Z" Sector on the German Plans for the invasion of England. The Chairman on that occasion, Col. Ambrose Keevil, announced that the General intended to enter a nursing home that day, but had postponed it in order to give his promised lecture. Those of us who were privileged to hear General

Brownrigg speak that evening carry with us the memory of the man as we saw him then; alert and full of vigour, a master of his subject, and a true patriot. The Home Guard of "Z" Sector will always remember him with affection and regard.

"Among Men"
By Pte. N. J. Fishlock

Four long years of your life—it's a sizeable span;
And you haven't done much, though you've done all you can.
This Home Guard, though—it's made you feel more like a man
    Yes, that's it: like a man, among men.

When officialdom's pen took the edge off the sword,
Many times you were weary, heart-sick of it, bored,
Wasting time—yes, and strength—that you couldn't afford.
    Yet you felt like a man, among men.

In a dark-dripping trench, missing sleep you had earned,
And above, a grim throbbing wherever you turned,
While away to the north London sullenly burned,
    You felt glad you were there, among men.

You left a bright fire and went out through the murk,
And you did a night's guard to round off a day's work.
You can't boast of an Arnhem, Dieppe or Dunkirk;
    But you felt like a man, among men.

Duty-nights in the guard-room, when training was done,
Drinking tea, swapping yarns, cursing, grousing like fun;
"The Sergeant? Who's he? The big- bachelor's son!"
    You felt good, like a man, among men.

It is midnight and cold, and the guard-room is still,
Then the siren—a fly-bomb comes over the hill!
Thoughts leap home—then a pal says: "Here, have a fag, Bill!
    And you're glad that you're there, among men.

Six o'clock in the morning, unshaven and dirty,
Stiff of body, blear-eyed, and inclined to be shirty—
You hear: "Don't be late, lad"—"Okay, Seven-thirty!"
    And you know that you're still among men.

Yes, you cursed and you blinded, and tempers grew shorter,
And the Sergeant mistook you for some kind of porter . . .
You'd have followed that man, though, through hell and high water,
    And felt proud to be there, among men!

Four years out of life we gave up, you and I;
But we've gained a few things that no money can buy.
This spirit, this comradeship, this must not die—
    It must live as a force, among men!

CHAPTER FOURTEEN

Contributed by Companies

JUST AS EVERY MEMBER of the 58th was fully convinced that his Battalion was the best in the Sector, so the members of each Company were of opinion that beyond any shadow of doubt theirs was the finest in the Battalion. There was thus five best Companies, each as proud of its reputation as any of the separate States of the U.S.A. The following notes contributed by members of the respective Companies show that each had reason to be proud of its record.

"A" Company

In May, 1940, when the L.D.V. were formed, "A" Company came into existence and was known as sub-Zone L.D.V. (London Area) Carshalton "Z" Zone.

The initial work of forming the Carshalton contingent was delegated to Mr. Daniel Thompson, a local business man who devoted himself whole-heartedly to the task. Under his energetic leadership the sub-Zone was quickly started, volunteers enrolled and training and guards commenced. Those who worked with him at the time pay tribute to his untiring efforts and realise it was entirely due to the latter that the sub-Zone received a flying start. Meetings were held at Mr. Thompson's offices and the district divided into four groups (subsequently called Platoons), Capt. D. L. Waghorn, M.C., D.C.M., Mr. F. G. Collins, Mr. W. Osborne and Mr. E. G. Tyler being appointed Group Commanders.

When the Battalion system was introduced, Carshalton sub-Zone became "D" Company No. 3 (Croydon) Battalion (afterwards 60th Surrey Battalion), by which time the title of L.D.V. had been changed to the Home Guard.

Shortly afterwards Mr. Thompson was transferred to Battalion Headquarters, first as Quartermaster and latterly Transport Officer. On August 6th, 1940, Capt. Waghorn became O/C Company, and when Home Guard commissions were instituted was granted the rank of Major with Capt. A. L. Pash, M.C., as Second-in-Command, and Lts. Boston, D.C.M., Collins, Barnes and Nanson as Platoon Commanders.

[*Photograph by E. F. Phillips.*
"A" COMPANY ON THE MARCH AT CARSHALTON—MAY, 1943.

On January 1st, 1941, another change was made; a re-organisation of Battalions had become necessary and "D" Company was transferred to the 58th, becoming "A" Company of that unit and the Platoons re-numbered 1, 2, 3, and 4 respectively.

Major Waghorn left to join the Regular Army in August, 1942, Capt. Pash being promoted Major and Company Commander in his stead with Capt. F. G. Collins as Second-in-Command, Lt. Launchbury taking over No. 2 Platoon. Major Pash had a distinguished career in the First World War in the Queen's Royal Regt., gaining the Military Cross and bar, with a long spell as a Company Commander in France. Under his guidance the Company made rapid progress.

"A" Company worthily upheld the high standard set by the 58th as witnessed by the following results of Battalion competitions. In the Inter-Platoon Marching and Shooting competition held on June 15th, 1941, No. 4 Platoon gained first place and No. 3 Platoon second, Nos. 1 and 2 Platoons gaining sixth and eleventh places respectively. The Battalion Miniature range competition held in May and June, 1944, was won by No. 4 Platoon with No. 3 second, No. 1 fourth and No. 2 fifth.

The Company always maintained a high standard of efficiency in rifle shooting, automatic and other weapons, and fifty-four Proficiency badges and 166 badges and bars were awarded to its members, and eighty-two certificates in various subjects were gained by its N.C.O's.

The strength of the Company was 285 for all ranks at its peak with a further twenty-five from the affiliated Works unit at the British Industrial Solvents, commanded by Lt. P. D. Wright.

In competitions within the Company, No. 4 Platoon won the "Waghorn" trophy of Miniature Range firing on the first shoot on May 23rd, 1942, and No. 1, who were runners-up on that occasion won this competition on December 3rd, 1943, with the former winners as runners-up. Two competitions were held on the open range for "A" and "B" teams in 1944, No. 1 Platoon winning both shoots. In the summer of 1944 a Platoon Efficiency test was held embodying most branches of training. No. 4 Platoon gained first place with No. 1 a close second, a few points only separating the other Platoons.

Much of the credit for the progress of the Company must be attributed to the sterling work of a fine body of N.C.O's, notably C.S.M. Scott, in the training of N.C.O's and recruits, C.Q.M.S. McClelland, M.M., for the efficient running of the Company Stores, etc., Armourer Sgt. W. A. Cobb for his instruction in various weapons and the supervision of arms and ammunition, Sgt. G. S. Wilson, Machine gun instructor and Sgt. Nelson for the training of the Signal Section.

Certificates for Meritorious Service were awarded to C.S.M. Scott, Sgt. Cobb and Sgt. Huckwell.

During the period of the flying bombs the Company turned out and rendered assistance to the victims at fifteen incidents, visiting most of them on two or three occasions.

"B" Company

"B" Company was formed from volunteers living in the Woodcote area of Purley who were enrolled by sub-Zone Organiser, Capt. Bruce Humfrey, J.P., Recorder of Croydon, two of his assistants who afterwards served with the Company, being A. J. Chapman (in command until appointed Assistant Zone Commander) and L. W. Ward, who took over command from Major Chapman. Enrolment took place at Croydon County Court, where Capt. Bruce Humfrey placed his Jury Room at the disposal of the L.D.V.

By the aid of a local house agent's map the Company area was divided into four Sections, and each of these Sectional localities eventually became Platoon areas for Nos. 5, 6, 7 and 8 Platoons. Recruits were posted to the sections in which they resided, and care was taken to exclude many who wished to volunteer but had previously enrolled in various branches of the Civil Defence services as it was considered both unfair and inexpedient to deplete those services.

Several hundred volunteers were quickly enrolled and the first operational posts manned within a few days of Mr. Anthony Eden's wireless appeal. Rifles were issued by the police to early volunteers, others brought along a miscellaneous collection of weapons, shot guns and revolvers, antique pistols and trophy weapons for which no ammunition could have possibly existed, and even old swords and bayonets—no one troubled what the weapon was so long as it was of an "offensive" nature.

Posts consisting of three men, one armed with a rifle, another with a "fancy" weapon, and the third with cycle or car, were placed in what was then considered the most advantageous positions to guard the approaches to the Company area; they were warned to be ceaselessly vigilant and make frequent contact with the nearest police officer or warden, and to locate telephones that could be used for communication in case of need.

[*Photograph by E. F. Phillips.*
"B" COMPANY PARADE AT WOODCOTE VILLAGE GREEN.

Tools for digging slit trenches were borrowed and Observation posts gradually established, many of which became official as time went on and were in use up to the time of "Stand Down". Before very long denim uniform was issued and gradually the insatiable desire of the many old soldiers for drills and musketry instruction led to regularly organised parades and lectures for those purposes. The spirit of loyalty and good citizenship which activated those original Volunteers was the foundation upon which "B" Company was built and that spirit remained to the end.

When commissions were granted A. J. Chapman became Major and Company Commander with Capt. Ward as his Second-in-Command, and when Major Chapman was promoted Lt.-Col. and Assistant Zone Commander, Capt. Ward became Major and Company Commander, the original Platoon Officers being Lt. Hutchins (No. 5), Lt. Ashby (No. 6), Lt. Newton (No. 7) and Lt. Williams (No. 8). In course of time these officers either left the Company or received Battalion appointments and the officer ranks in Platoons were as follows:—No. 5, Lt. Anderson in Command with Lt. Cooke, M.C., as Second-in-Command; No. 6, Lt. G. Reeve, M.C., in Command with Lt. D. Leck, M.C., as Second-in-Command; No. 7, Lt. J. Lamb in Command with Lt. Lloyd as Second-in-Command; and No. 8, Lt. T. Hague in Command with Lt. W. Morgan as Second-in-Command.

The Company also furnished Battalion with the following Headquarters Staff:—Major Brewer, O/C Headquarters Company; Capt. Bryant, Weapon Training Officer; Lt. Grant, M.M., Assistant Adjutant; Lt. Williams, Cadet Liaison Officer; Lt. Fouraker, Anti-Gas Officer; Lt. Clutterbuck, M.M., Ammunition Officer; Lt. Fitton, Transport Officer; and Lt. Povey, Bombing Officer; in addition to which C.S.M. Appleton was appointed R.S.M. of the Battalion.

The Company took an active part in all Battalion events and from first to last provided the nightly guard on Battalion Headquarters. These duties were not always without incident, as has been related in an earlier chapter of this history.

The record of the Company, both of Proficiency badges and Sector Instructor's certificates, was an excellent one. In numbers at "Stand Down" it exceeded 300, with an additional twenty-six members from the East Surrey Water Company and twenty-nine from the British Overseas Airways Corporation, which were attached for training and administration. The Company was responsible for the defence of many important roads and built-up localities, also of vital open spaces.

Most of the men came from the Purley area and the Company was therefore regarded as Purley's own citizen force. It was a smart well-trained Company and deserved all the praise it received.

During the heavy bombing attacks in the locality members did splendid work, as they also did during the flying bomb period, rendering every assistance possible both to the Police and Civil Defence services. Throughout the whole of its existence the Company lived up to the Battalion motto—"Service not Self".

"C" and "D" Companies

The sub-Zone of the L.D.V. enrolled in Coulsdon was divided into Eastern and Western sectors, the former comprising Purley (south of Godstone Road), Kenley and Whyteleafe under W. C. Dodkins, the Western Sector under L. Plowman, including the remainder of the Company Area—Brighton Road (from Old Lodge Lane), Coulsdon and Old Coulsdon. A certain amount of overlapping was unavoidable. Together these two sectors formed "C" Company of No. 1 Purley Battalion, "Z" Zone, under the command of Capt. R. G. Hudson, with headquarters in Brighton Road, Coulsdon.

In Company Orders dated February 16th, 1941, it was stated that authority had been received for Eastern sector to be known in future as "D" Company, Western Sector becoming "C" Company, both remaining under the command of Capt. R. G. Hudson and being administered as a double-Company.

It was during this adolescence of "C" Company that Platoon Commander W. Battle (Eastern Sector) was killed by a bomb while on duty at Kenley on August 18th, 1940—the only fatal casualty due to enemy action in the Battalion. This was the first daylight raid on the Battalion area.

The period between the enrolment of the first L.D.V. Volunteer at Brighton Road and the change of name to Home Guard in the autumn of 1940 saw a gradual building up of an organisation, and the beginning of a trickle of equipment. By the time subsistence allowance was granted to the Home Guard, "C" Company had acquired an "Assistant Adjutant", Capt. F. C. Crosse (an entirely unofficial appointment), a strength of over 500, a certain amount of office staff (honorary, unpaid and of fluctuating quantity), new headquarters at 69 Brighton Road, and a Quartermaster—Vol. R. Jones—to deal with the equipment and stores as and when they materialised. The Company even had a D.R., Vol. Elkins, who called at Battalion Headquarters for Orders, Amendments of, and Cancellations. At this time there were two C.S.M's—Vol. Sattler, (subsequently transferred to "D" Company), for administration, and Vol. James, who became C.S.M. "C" Company when "D" Company eventually became a separate entity.

[*Photograph by E. F. Phillips.*
"C" COMPANY GIVE A DEMONSTRATION.

During the summer of 1940 "C" Company undertook the first ceremonial parade of the 58th, a Guard of Honour under Platoon Commander Hullett being provided by the Cane Hill Platoon when the Zone Commander, Major-General Anderson, whose advent was much delayed by Croydon's first air raid then in progress, addressed the Company at Cane Hill. This performance vividly reminded "old sweats" of one of the 1914-1918 Army's favourite marching songs—"We are Fred Karno's Army".

In 1941, building up, reorganisation, equipment, and training, were the main items on the programme. Early in the year the original "C" Company was split into two Companies "C" and "D", commanded respectively by Majors L. Plowman and W. C. Dodkins. Major Hudson becoming Second-in-Command of the Battalion. This operation caused many headaches and arguments in the two quartermastering departments regarding the apportionment of the available equipment and stores. The conversion of Eastern Sector into "D" Company did not solve all "C" Company's geographical problems. Unlike ancient Gaul the Company area was divided into two parts—the Highlands (Old Coulsdon and Farthing Down), referred to as "up top" by aboriginal inhabitants, and the comparative Lowlands of Brighton Road, Coulsdon. Nos. 11 and 12 Platoons constituted the Highlanders, Nos. 9 and 10 being located in the Lowlands with Headquarters in The Avenue, and The Grove, Coulsdon, respectively.

The separation of the Companies did not sever the bonds of comradeship forged during their service together in those early anxious months of the L.D.V.'s existence, when enemy parachutists were expected whenever the weather was favourable. Orders issued at that time show how real the danger was thought to be. Section Leaders were required, in the event of enemy action, "to defend their rear by turning about at least one rifleman ready to deal with a possible fifth column", and Orders went on to remind them of the necessity for extreme vigilance "as the enemy can get to this area in twenty-two minutes from his bases in France".

Major L. Plowman, an Artillery Officer of the First World War, who commanded "C" Company, had as his Second-in-Command Capt. E. J. Brown, who had served with a Territorial Battalion of the Queen's Royal Regiment before, during, and after that war. The Officers who served in the Company's four Platoons, (9, 10, 11, and 12) were as follows (Platoon Commanders being in italics); Lts. *H. W. N. Creal* (relinquished commission) *F. W. Hullett*, F. C. Mair, W. G. St. L. Montague (transferred to Battalion as Signals Officer). *C. A. O'Neill* (relinquished commission), J. E.

Nelson (transferred to Battalion), *G. W. Nickerson*, B. D. Parmenter (deceased), C. A. Pratt, C. V. Rich, *L. Smetham, K. N. Wilcockson*, and 2/Lt. R. H. Goodman.

By slow degrees in 1941 and 1942 the Home Guard, including "C" Company, became more and more military. Real uniforms began to take the place of denims, weapons, including the famous pikes, became in less short supply, the original gentle flow of paper between the various headquarters swelled to a raging flood; courses of instruction for Officers and Other Ranks multiplied; "volunteers" were transformed into Sergeants, Corporals, Lance-Corporals, and Privates, and the Platoon Commanders of L.D.V. days blossomed into commissioned Officers. In a word the Home Guard had become part of the Armed Forces. Home-made bombs became a memory. The "back-room boys" produced new and fearful weapons for the use of the spare-time soldier, and "C" Company had its share of the spoils—Vickers and Browning heavy machine-guns, Lewis guns, Flame Fougasses, Spigot mortars, Tommy-guns, Northover Projectors, Automatic rifles, Stens, Smith guns, and finally two-pounder anti-tank guns, were all examined, stripped, re-assembled, and inwardly digested by those detailed to deal with them.

During these two years, while "C" Company was growing up, many changes took place. Owing to ill-health Private Jones moved from the Quartermaster's Stores to Company Office to concentrate upon records, his place as C.Q.M.S. being taken by Sgt. F. A. Savage of No. 12 Platoon. "Snowballs" were invented as a means of calling out the Company quickly in an emergency. As the flow of voluntary recruits dried up, direction of men into the Home Guard was instituted. The various Orders issued were revised and collected into two printed volumes of Home Guard Regulations, which were subsequently amended, re-amended, and cancelled almost out of recognition. There were days at Bisley, camps, all-night exercises, rumours of Proficiency badges. The "Fred Karno" period had definitely come to an end.

In January, 1943, Company Headquarters was moved from Brighton Road to Marlpit Drill Hall—a brand new building fitted with every modern convenience. Instead of sitting on one another's laps the Administrative staff found themselves installed in a palatial panelled room from which, subsequently, a grandstand view was obtained of passing flying bombs and the balloon barrage. As a result of this removal "C" Company became the envy of the Battalion. No other Company enjoyed such accommodation, and "C" made full use of it, as did the Battalion for Proficiency badge examinations, and Sector for a popular series of week-end camps, the large number of men attending for instruction being accommodated in the hutments adjoining the spacious parade ground, upon which the final "Stand Down" parade of the Battalion was ultimately held.

Not only had the Company scope to carry out its military training under ideal conditions, but opportunity was given for organising some excellent concerts and dances, to the considerable advantage of local charities. Both in its work and social activities the Company set the same high standard; it had a fine record of successes in Battalion competitions and gained a large number of Proficiency badges and Sector Instructors' certificates. In one or two respects "C" Company was probably unique in the Battalion.

From July, 1940, the Company had a Recruit Training squad in charge of Sgt. Instructor J. R. Raindle, to which all newly-enrolled men were posted, and from which they were in due course "passed out" to the Platoons. Their stamping ground was the Harrier's Hall, Coulsdon, and the fields of Cane Hill Hospital. Early in its history the Company had a section of Pioneers, but they eventually faded away. For a considerable time it had enough D.R's (complete with own motorcycles) to run a rota of one duty night per week per D.R. Owing to men being called up the personnel changed, but the service kept well up to strength until "Stand Down". Cpl. G. W. Ford (No. 10 Platoon) set up a Battalion and Sector record in his Proficiency badge examination by obtaining 100 per cent. marks.

The Company recruited few Women Auxiliaries, but one— Mrs. Jenkins—typed and duplicated the Company Orders from the first in 1940 to the last on December 5th, 1944. From first to last over 1,100 men were enrolled in the Company.

In 1943 and 1944 training continued without major incident, though of the many minor ones which served to enliven the routine, such as the surprising flight from the spigot of what was thought to be a 14 lb. drill bomb, space does not permit a record. Then came the Spring of 1944, when the approach of "D" Day brought about changes. Company Headquarters then became a temporary resting place for various units of the Army on their way South prior to the landing in Normandy, not without profit to the Company both in the way of extra training and the acquisition of unconsidered trifles of spare ammunition.

As soon as the P.A.C. (*alias* flying bomb) made its appearance the various Platoons were on call to assist the Civil Defence at "incidents" in the Company area, and turned out in strength to lend their aid in clearing away debris and carrying out first-aid repairs. A liberal interpretation of this expression to include the complete re-tiling of a whole street earned for the Company the gratitude of local residents, except in the case of one very independent old lady who, when asked if she would like her shattered windows repaired, replied "that when she wanted the Home Guard she would send for it". Perhaps it was fortunate that the "Stand Down" came just a day after the last flying bomb incident in the Battalion area.

At the time of its constitution as a separate Company "D" was commanded by Major Dodkins with Capt. S. F. Wood as Second-in-Command. Headquarters had been established at a garage in Burcott Road, Purley, placed at its disposal by Mr. P. E. Ridley, a local resident to whom the Company was indebted for many acts of kindness. Seldom has the garage of a private residence been the scene of greater activity; for over a year, until a house in Higher Drive was requisitioned in June, 1941, it was Orderly Room, Stores, and lecture room combined. Capt. Wood, a veteran of the South African and first world wars, in which latter he served with the Worcestershire Regiment, was one of the first to enrol in May, 1940, although well over military age, and partially crippled by a severe wound which caused his discharge from the Army in 1919 and prevented his becoming an active member of the L.D.V. By taking over the administration of the Company, where his considerable experience was invaluable, he enabled the Company Commander to devote far more time to organisation and training than would otherwise have been possible. In this capacity he rendered splendid service until his health began to fail towards the end of 1943, and although obliged to resign his commission through ill-health in June, 1944, he remained on the strength of the Battalion until "Stand Down". A fine record, and the writer pays this tribute to a comrade who was always willing to work beyond his physical strength "for the good of the cause".

When Company Headquarters moved to Higher Drive the garage was fitted up as a Casualty Collecting Post and became a centre for first-aid training. During the various tactical exercises and frequent alarms it was fully manned, as also was another garage used for a similar purpose in Welcomes Road, Kenley, by ladies who volunteered their services long before Women Auxiliaries were authorised.

After Capt. Wood relinquished his appointment, Lt. C. R. Burvill, senior subaltern, was promoted Captain and Second-in-Command. One of the original members of Kenley Platoon he had brought it to a high state of efficiency and was a popular and extremely capable officer. Company Sgt. Major J. E. Hobbs was appointed to a commission as Lieutenant and took charge of the

["Croydon Times" Photograph.
"D" Company's Inspection at Kenley—May, 1941.

facing page 56

58TH SURREY HOME GUARD

Orderly Room at Company Headquarters. He was another who willingly took over any job to help the Company and made a success of them all.

At first the Company consisted of Headquarters and three Platoons only, Nos. 13, 14, and 15, but No. 13 grew in numbers and by July, 1941, exceeded the establishment so was divided into Nos. 13 and 14, the other Platoons being renumbered 15 and 16 respectively. As only two of them were drawn from "built-up" areas the Company was rather smaller than the others, numbering about 250 of all ranks at "Stand Down", but what it lacked in numbers it made up in enthusiasm as shown by the high percentage of men who never failed to answer the roll.

The Officers of No. 13 (Reedham) were Lts. A. G. Grisenthwaite and F. S. E. May; of No. 14 (South-east Purley) Lts. J. G. M. Allan and E. Clarke, who subsequently became Battalion Camouflage Officer; of N. 15 (Kenley) Lts. L. Weightman and C. R. Burvill, and of No. 16 (Whyteleafe) Lts. P. G. Burgess and D. W. Macfarlane. When Lt. Weightman was transferred to Battalion as Intelligence and Liaison Officer Lt. Burvill took over No. 15 with Lt. A. M. Brougham Platoon Officer, and after Lt. Burvill became Second-in-Command of the Company, the Platoon was commanded by Lt. Brougham with 2/Lt. G. L. Day as his deputy. In the early days of the L.D.V., before military ranks were authorised and all were known as "volunteers", the Kenley Platoon was in charge of William Battle, whose death at his post during an air raid in August, 1940, is recorded earlier in this narrative. Mr. Weightman then acted as Second-in-Command.

The Warrant Officers and N.C.O's were dependable and efficient. C.S.M. Clark, a fine soldier whose son was "one of the boys of the 58th" until he became a pilot in the Fleet Air Arm, rendered outstanding service to the Company. He was unfortunately incapacitated by an accident sustained while on duty in July, 1943, and was succeeded by P/Sgt. Hobbs of No. 13 Platoon. Upon the appointment of the latter to a commission, P/Sgt. Barker of No. 16 Platoon became Company Sergt. Major and worthily upheld the traditions of his rank. C.Q.M.S. Johnson, M.B.E., had spent an adventurous life in the Regular Army and Sudan Government Service, and made a name as a big game hunter. As a Quartermaster he proved a master of the art, his stores and records a model of efficiency. Armourer Sgt. Holdsworth kept rifles and automatic weapons in serviceable condition and did consistently good work both at Headquarters and on the ranges.

In the Home Guard Platoon Sergeants were very valuable N.C.O's and had responsible duties. A. S. Moore of No. 13,

A. G. Griffiths, M.C., of No. 14, A. H. Collins of No. 15 and A. E. Pearce of No. 16, did their work efficiently and well.

By its Section Sergeants, Corporals and Lance-Corporals, the Company was equally well served. Together they forged a Company which, like their Battalion, they considered second to none.

Company Headquarters also served as the Headquarters of Nos. 13 and 14 Platoons, and a local hall was obtained for their winter training. A school at Kenley provided Headquarters for No. 15 and an empty shop at Whyteleafe accommodated No. 16. Higher Drive Recreation Ground and the grounds of St. Winifred's, Kenley, for which latter the Company was indebted to the Phoenix Assurance Company Limited, gave facilities for outdoor training. Each Platoon paraded two evenings a week. Sunday mornings were devoted either to Company or Platoon training. Musketry and Grenade practices were held on various ranges either Saturday afternoons or Sunday mornings. In addition, Guard Duty fell to each member by rota approximately one night in eight, although in 1940 and 1941 it was sometimes nearer one night in five. Officers, W.O's and Sergeants had additional duties—in fact they did not have an idle moment. But in spite of it, there was not one of them unwilling to take on still another job if it would help things along. Their loyalty and devotion to the Home Guard was as great as their pride in their Company; they were men with whom it was an honour to serve.

No reference to St. Winifred's should omit the fact that it was the scene of a noteworthy example of "group enlistment" into the L.D.V. During the first week of the war the Phoenix Assurance Company Ltd., migrated a large part of its City staff to a previously earmarked Preparatory school at that address. Thirty employees who lived North of the Thames were billeted on the premises and saw their homes only at week-ends. Twenty of these immediately offered their services *en bloc* and were enrolled in a body by Capt. R. G. Hudson.

Thereafter, under the guiding hand of Mr. L. Weightman—one of the Managers of the Company, who subsequently graduated from Platoon Commander to Battalion Intelligence and Liaison Officer—this compact unit of underwriting soldiers proceeded upon a self-imposed training programme (there were no Home Guard Instructions in those days) using its own private parade ground, miniature rifle range, lecture room and armoury of privately-owned weapons. The inspection of "D" Company by Major-General Anderson in the grounds of St. Winifred's in May, 1941, provided one of its red-letter days.

The Phoenix unit inevitably became merged into No. 15 Platoon of "D" Company, and certain of its members were still on the Company roll when the Assurance Company's staff was recalled to London in November, 1944.

On Sunday, May 18th, 1941, three months after its separation from "C", "D" Company was inspected by the late Major-General N. G. Anderson, Zone Commander, and Lt.-Col. R. L. Haine, v.c., m.c., Commanding Officer of the Battalion. It has been said its appearance and work on this occasion put the newly-formed Company on the map; it had certainly reached a stage of efficiency that more than satisfied the inspecting Officers.

Its subsequent history was the history of the Battalion. For four-and-a-half years it took part in all the latter's activities for which there was never a lack of volunteers. It had a good record and played a worthy part in building up the Battalion's reputation. It gained a considerable number of Proficiency badges and Sector Instructor's certificates. It furnished Battalion with some first-class specialist Officers, notably Capt. Weightman, Battalion Intelligence and Liaison Officer; Lt. Peacock, m.m., Signals Officer; Lt. Clarke, Camouflage Officer, and Lt. Woodroof, Borough Military Liaison Officer, all of whom served with credit.

The Company turned out on many occasions during the "flying bomb" period, and like every other in the Battalion, did its best for the unfortunate victims.

Reference has already been made to the ladies who manned the Casualty Collecting Posts. There were others whose help was also greatly appreciated; first, the Women Auxiliaries who, enthusiastic and quick to learn, were an acquisition to the Signals staff and did good work during many important tactical exercises. Last, but not least, Mrs. Edgar Ridley, wife of one of our members, who typed Company Orders for the first year of our service, and Mrs. D. H. Scott, our very efficient Company clerk and typist from June, 1941, until "Stand Down".

Headquarters Company and Mobile Reserve

Headquarters Company was formed early in 1941 under the command of Major H. C. Brewer, a former Officer of the London Scottish. It consisted of the personnel attached to Battalion Headquarters, signallers, transport, etc., also the Battalion Mobile Reserve which was incorporated into Headquarters Company upon its formation in July, 1942. The latter was under the direct command of Capt. W. R. McIntosh and had a separate Headquarters at "Strathclyde", Purley. Lt. R. K. May acted as Second-in-Command of Mobile Reserve, Lt. R. A. Waine, M.M., was a Platoon commander and 2/Lt. S. W. Pruden a Platoon Officer.

The following specialist Officers were attached to this Company at "Stand Down":—

Major L. Meakin	Medical Officer
Capt. A. L. Bryant	Weapon Training
Capt. L. Weightman	Liaison
Lt. E. Clarke	Camouflage
Lt. H. S. F. Clutterbuck, M.M.	Ammunition
Lt. A. J. Fitton	Motor Transport
Lt. E. H. Fouraker	Anti-Gas Training
Lt. J. Gates	Borough Military Liaison
Lt. F. A. Grant, M.M.	Assistant Adjutant
Lt. W. Peacock, M.M.	Signals
Lt. W. M. Whiteman	Intelligence and Security
Lt. W. J. Williams	Cadet Training
Lt. F. J. Woodroof	Borough Military Liaison
2/Lt. R. J. Brown	Physical Training
2/Lt. C. B. Povey	Bombing

With the exception of the Company Commander, who also acted as Sector Bombing Officer and, as such, was responsible for the training of all Bombing Officers throughout the Sector, the Officers of the Mobile Reserve, and the Battalion Medical Officer, all specialist Officers were transferred from Companies at various periods.

Their work often entailed many hours of duty at a time, but like every other Officer of the 58th, they gave of their best to their particular job. They were a fine team of specialists and the Companies owed a debt of gratitude to them.

The excellent work of some has already been mentioned but all were equally deserving. Lt. Fitton could always be depended upon to provide something in the way of transport; his Section and the P.S.I's kept the W.D. vehicles in first-class condition and responded to every call made upon them. Lt. Fouraker never failed to make his Gas lectures interesting and could hold the close attention of his audiences—a great feat, as there were many subjects far more popular. Lt. Peacock performed miracles with a few coils of obsolete telephone wire, and accepted orders to connect up posts miles apart with as much unconcern as if he had the whole resources of the Royal Signals at his command.

One and all they played a part in the making of an efficient Battalion.

A word about the Mobile Reserve; known throughout the Battalion as a "good crowd", they were of an average age rather younger than the Companies and specially trained for mobility.

[Photograph by E. F. Phillips.

MOBILE RESERVE—THE "KING'S" DETACHMENT.

Their function to move rapidly to any part of the Battalion area where they might be required; their speciality attack and counterattack. On schemes and tactical exercises they invariably managed to put up a good show, and in the event of an enemy landing would have been invaluable.

Finally an appreciation of the work of those at Battalion Headquarters. In the preceding pages reference has been made to the Adjutant, Quartermaster, R.S.M., and R.Q.M.S., as well as to the two Permanent Staff Instructors. All of them went out of their way to give the Companies practical help, advice, and information. With the word "information" most Company Officers will associate Miss Joan Raper, a member of the small but efficient clerical staff, who had an amazing memory and was a veritable encyclopædia of information.

The Home Guard

by Lt. John Gates

In Britain's darkest hour, when all the world
Counted her humbled, beaten to her knees,
　The call went forth for men to hold the breach
And keep the Land they loved inviolate.

　To back the proud defiance Churchill hurled
That he would never yield, not on the seas,
　Nor on the land, but fight upon the beach,
And on the hills, and at the City's gate.

　Scarce was the airborne voice of Eden mute,
Then floodgates opened and a swelling stream
　Of men poured forth, ready to serve, to die,
If fate so willed, so long as England stood.

　This then was Britain's answer to the Brute,
Who drunk with conquest thought to reign supreme
　Over the Earth, the Seas, and in the Sky;
All Nations subject to his hell-hatched brood;

　Old men and young men, others in their prime,
Many of them veterans of other wars,
　Men of every calling, working all day long,
Giving up their leisure, learning how to fight.

　These were the Home Guard, who in course of time
Grew into an army fit to guard our shores.
　Well armed and confident, spirited, and strong,
In readiness for action day or night.

　The last fall in has sounded for the Passing Out Parade,
For the danger we'd to guard against has passed,
　But, please God, we'll keep and cherish the friendships
　　　　　　　　　　　　　　　we have made.
Till we fall in for inspection at the Last Great Trumpet Blast.

[*Photograph by A. W. Kerr.*
OFFICERS OF THE 58TH AT "STAND DOWN".

AN APPEAL
TO
My Comrades of the 58th

IN THIS LITTLE BOOK I have tried to tell the story of our Battalion. If it brings back to your memories some of the happy times we spent together, and our wonderful comradeship, you will, I hope, overlook its imperfections and not think unkindly of the writer.

The delay in publication is due to causes beyond my control. Some may wonder why the positions of their defence posts and anti-tank barriers have not been given, but for security reasons it is still impossible to make public certain types of military information.

Any profit from the sale of the book will go to the Old Comrades' Association Benevolent Fund, which, very quietly and unobtrusively, has been doing splendid work since the Battalion was "stood down". Most of you will have heard little or nothing of its activities, and because you have heard nothing, thought it was doing nothing, but many old comrades, stricken by illness or hardship, have been helped, quickly and generously, by the contributions you were kind enough to make to the fund while we were serving together. Employment has been found for many members; sometimes for their sons. Temporary help has been given to ex-service comrades until their circumstances could be brought to the notice of the British Legion. No case of suffering or distress has ever been turned down, nor ever will be so long as we are in a position to help.

This is a cause very close to my heart! I will tell you of one case—one of many. I heard that an ex-service member of my old Company was very ill and in hospital. I went to see him and took him a few cigarettes and something to read. He was dying of cancer, but had no fear for himself; his one anxiety was his wife, elderly, delicate, and partially blind. We talked together and I promised him she should never want; we would see her through. His time was short and he knew it, but his last hours were comforted by the thought that he had someone to turn to in his distress. He died and we have not failed him. When I say "we", I mean "you"—his old comrades.

You and I often read of "quotas" and goods in short supply. Put yourself in the place of a man whose job suddenly closed down because of lack of materials. Who for the first time in his life found himself unable to pay his housekeeping bills, and faced with a milkman who refused to serve him again until his debt was paid. There he was, worried and anxious, with not even the consolation of a cup of tea. He asked nobody's help—we are a proud lot in the 58th—but the news got round that old so-and-so was "up against it", and it was brought to the notice of the Benevolent Fund. Their response was prompt and effective. Old so-and-so now has his cup of tea—and he has another job as well.

Some of us were not so young when we joined the Battalion; as we get older more will require a helping hand. I ask you to make it possible. In the Battle of Britain it was the few who saved the many. In this case it is the many who are saving the few. If you can send a donation, or know of a job going, you may be the means of helping an old comrade to continue his fight for the battle of life, a battle which some are finding very hard these days, remembering always that but for the grace of God the one in need might be you—or me.

Our Hon. Secretary is Mr. S. L. Fulker, of 50 The Chase, Coulsdon (UPLANDS 3015). He is doing a fine job and every penny you send him will be devoted to the cause—every penny will pay a dividend in human happiness. Let him know, also, the name and address of any old member in want or distress; he will go and see them with five pounds in his pocket, then he will suggest to your Committee, upon which most Platoons are represented, what else can be done.

Now it is up to you!

Thanks for your help; I know I shall not ask in vain.

W. C. DODKINS.

OFFICERS OF THE 58TH AT 'STAND DOWN'.

Left to Right. On ground: Lt. W. H. Weatley, T. A. Nanson, F. J. Woodroof, H. G. Grisenthwaite, J. G. Allan, Capt. A. S. McFarlane (M.O.),
Front Row: Capt. E. J. Brown, Capt. P. C. Litchfield, M.C. (M.O.), Capt. H. C. Miller (Adjt.), Majors L. W. Ward, A. L. Pash, M.C., H. C. Brewer, Lt.-Col. R. L. Haine, V.C., M.C. (C.O.), Majors L. Plowman, W. C. Dodkins, L. Meakin (M.O.), Capts. R. E. Godfrey (Q.M.), A. L. Bryant, F. G. Collins.
Second Row: Capt. C. R. Burvill, Capt. J. B. Browning, M.C., Lts. D. H. Leck, M.C., L. Smetham, A. J. Fitton, G. R. Reeve, M.C., R. K. May, E. H. Fouraker, W. Peacock, M.M., W. R. Pullen, G. G. Boston, D.C.M., H. Clutterbuck, M.M., A. D. Anderson, P. G. R. Burgess, J. E. Hobbs, Capt. W. R. McIntosh.
Third Row: Lts. J. C. Lamb, F. S. E. May, F. A. Grant, M.M., T. W. Hague, W. A. G. Morgan, A. M. Brougham, 2/Lt. R. J. Brown, Lt. W. J. Williams, Lt. D. G. Cooke, M.C., 2/Lt. G. A. Day, Lt. G. E. Garrard, Lt. H. G. Launchbury.
Back Row: Lt. J. Gates, Lt. P. D. Wright, 2/Lt. C. B. Povey, M.M., Lts. K. N. Wilcockson, C. V. Rich, R. H. Goodman, F. C. Mair, C. A. Pratt, F. W. Hullett, C. F. Lloyd, A. I. R. Barnes, W. M. Whiteman, 2/Lt. S. W. Pruden, Lt. R. A. Waine, M.M., Lt. H. S. Crabtree.

Nominal Roll of Battalion
as at 3rd December, 1944

Officers

Haine, Lt. Col. R. L., v.c., m.c.
Hudson, Major R. G.

REGULAR ARMY STAFF

Miller, Capt. H. C.
Seaforth Highlanders

Godfrey, Capt. R. E.
Royal Artillery

HEADQUARTERS COMPANY

Brewer, Major H. C.
Brown, 2/Lt. R. J.
Bryant, Capt. A. L.
Clarke, Lt. E.
Clutterbuck, Lt. H. S. F., m.m.
Fitton, Lt. A. J.
Fouraker, Lt. E. H.
Gates, Lt. J.
Grant, Lt. F. A., m.m.
May, Lt. R. K.
Meakin, Major L.
McIntosh, Capt. W. R.
Peacock, Lt. W., m.m.
Povey, 2/Lt. C. B.
Pruden, 2/Lt. S. W.
Waine, Lt. R. A., m.m.
Weightman, Capt. L.
Whiteman, Lt. W. M.
Williams, Lt. W. J.
Woodroof, Lt. F. J.

'A' COMPANY

Barnes, Lt. A. R. I.
Boston, Lt. G. G., d.c.m.
Collins, Capt. F. G.
Hancock, Lt. H. L. W.
Knights, Lt. G. A.
Launchbury, Lt. H. G.
McFarlane, Capt. A. S.
Nanson, Lt. T. A.
Pash, Major A. L., m.c.
Pullen, Lt. W. R.
Wheatley, Lt. W. H.

'B' COMPANY

Anderson, Lt. A. D.
Browning, Capt. J. B., m.c.
Cooke, Lt. D. G., m.c.
Hague, Lt. T. W.
Lamb, Lt. J. C.
Leck, Lt. D. H., m.c.
Litchfield, Capt. P. C., m.c.
Lloyd, Lt. C. F.
Morgan, Lt. W. A. G.
Reeve, Lt. G. R., m.c.
Ward, Major L. W.

'C' COMPANY

Brown, Capt. E. J.
Goodman, 2/Lt. R. H.
Hullett, Lt. F. W.
Mair, Lt. F. C.
Nickerson, Lt. G. W.
Parmenter, Lt. B. D.
Plowman, Major L.
Pratt, Lt. C. A.
Rich, Lt. C. V.
Smetham, Lt. L.
Wilcockson, Lt. K. N.

'D' COMPANY

Allan, Lt. J. G. Mc. C.
Brougham, Lt. A. M.
Burgess, Lt. P. G. R.
Burvill, Capt. C. R.
Day, 2/Lt. G. L.
Dodkins, Major W. C.
Grisenthwaite, Lt. A. G.
Hobbs, Lt. J. E.
May, Lt. F. S. E.
Macfarlane, Lt. D. W.

BRITISH INDUSTRIAL SOLVENTS PLATOON
Wright, Lt. P. D.

EAST SURREY WATER COMPANY PLATOON
Garrard, Lt. G. E.

BRITISH OVERSEAS AIRWAYS CORPORATION PLATOON
Crabtree, Lt. H. S.

58TH SURREY HOME GUARD

Other Ranks

REGULAR ARMY STAFF

Goodsell, Sgt. A. V.
Royal Artillery

Langridge, Sgt. W.
Queen's Royal Regt.

HEADQUARTERS COMPANY

Allison, Pte. E.
Allison, Pte. R. G.
Antrobus, Pte. J. R.
Appleton, R.S.M. L. C.
Armitage, Pte. H. E.
Batterbury, L/Cpl. W. C.
Beasley, Pte. L. F.
Beck, Pte. A. H.
Birt, Pte. W. E.
Blank, Pte. E. A.
Blewett, Pte. J. H. T.
Blyth, Cpl. T. L.
Bosworth, Pte. V. C.
Bowden, Pte. T.
Brickwell, Pte. O. A.
Bridle, Pte. E. G.
Bromly, Pte. P. R.
Brown, Pte. D. R.
Brown, Cpl. H. L.
Brown, L/Cpl. P. R.
Butcher, Pte. E. W.
Byard, Pte. C. W.
Canham, Pte. L. J.
Carter, Cpl. W. F.
Cawley, Pte. C. G.
Clancy, Pte. T.
Clark, Sgt. G.
Codrington, Cpl. J. A. E.
Collins, Pte. D. M.
Cook, Pte. J. N.
Copping, Pte. G.
Cove, Sgt. E. G.
Cox, Pte. H. J.
Creber, Pte. F.
Crisell, Pte. A. E.
Crosse, Pte. F. C.
Cumings, Sgt. A. E.
Darlington, Pte. H. J.
David, Cpl. E. G.
Denton, Pte. C.
Fawcett, Pte. J.
Feeder, Pte. A.
Fenton, Pte. P. E. T.
Field, Cpl. W. T.
Goddard, Pte. C. N.
Goodayle, Pte. C. R.
Green, Pte. H. V.
Griffiths, L/Cpl. I. H.
Hall, Cpl. E. A.
Hammond, Pte. E. C.
Harris, Pte. L.
Harrison, R.Q.M.S. A. W.
D.C.M., M.M.

Hartley, Sgt. H. J.
Hayden, Cpl. R. L. J.
Heal, L/Cpl. C. H.
Hore, Pte. G. D.
Humphreys, Pte. C. N.
Humphreys, Pte. F.
Hunnybun, Pte. R. H. C.
Hunt, Pte. R. A. J.
Jonas, Pte. R. A.
Lee, Cpl. E. A.
Lilley, Sgt. L. G.
Lowman, Pte. A.
Mann, Pte. R. S.
March, Cpl. G. A.
Martin, Cpl. F. A.
Mawdsley, Pte. A. B.
Maynard, Pte. A.
Moore, Pte. G. R. E.
Moore, Pte. L. R.
Muschamp, Pte. L. N.
McNairn, Pte. E. S.
Nagle, Pte. C.
Nash, Pte. R. J.
Nickinson, Pte. H. D.
Nightingale, Pte. A. L.
Ockenden, Pte. N. S.
Parry, Pte. R. J.
Partridge, Pte. E. J.
Phillips, Pte. E. F.
Philpot, Pte. G. S.
Poole, Pte. G. H. W.
Poynter, Sgt. H. C.
Preston, Pte. H. E. R.
Price, Pte. A. H.
Price, L/Cpl. S. W.
Prior, Pte. E. G.
Pryer, Pte. K. A.
Pulham, Pte. C. A. B.
Rawkins, Pte. S. A.
Richards, Pte. G. E.
Richardson, Pte. W.
Robinson, Pte. D. T.
Rudge, Pte. P. E.
Samwell, Pte. L. G.
Sheridan, L/Cpl. S. F.
Smith, Pte. E. H.
Smith, Pte. L.
Smith, Pte. L. E. W.
Staddon, Pte. P. R. B.
Staddon, Pte. R. B.

58TH SURREY HOME GUARD

Stephens, Pte. T. R.
Stevens, Pte. J.
Thomas, L/Cpl. R. C.
Turnbull, Pte. F.
Turner, L/Cpl. E. A.
Tyler, Sgt. E. G.
Usill, Sgt. D. M.
Walpole, L/Cpl. A. E.
Watson, Pte. J. H. E.
Wells, Pte. H. J.

White, Pte. J.
Whiteside, L/Cpl. D. A.
Williamson, L/Cpl. A. E.
Wilson, L/Cpl. M. D., M.C.
Wood, L/Cpl. S. F.
Woodroy, L/Cpl. J. W.
Worringham, Sgt. C. H.
Wort, Cpl. B. G.
Youell, Pte. G. H.
Young, L/Cpl. A. D.
Young, Pte. J. J.

'A' COMPANY

Allam, Pte. P. F.
Anderson, Pte. B.
Anderson, Pte. J. T.
Angus, Pte. H. P.
Archer, Pte. L. G.
Armitage, Pte. C. D.
Baker, Pte. E. F.
Bailey, Pte. A. A.
Banks, Pte. E. H.
Barlow, Pte. J. H.
Barnes, Pte. F. W.
Bartlett, Pte. F. W.
Bayntun, Cpl. W.
Bean, Pte. A. H. F.
Beck, Pte. H. J.
Bolger, Pte. M. F.
Boty, Pte. A. A.
Bowles, Pte. J. L.
Bradbeer, Pte. F. E. W.
Brewster, Sgt. J. A.
Brooks, Pte. A. W.
Brown, Pte. R.
Brown, Cpl. R. A
Brownlow, Pte. J. H.
Burchell, Pte. L. C.
Bull, Pte. L. A.
Card, Pte. C.
Carthew, Pte. F. G.
Catt, L/Cpl. R.
Cavey, Pte. A. S.
Champion, Pte. G.
Chapman, Sgt C. E.
Chase, L/Cpl. L. N.
Cheney, Pte. E.
Cheyne, Pte. J. D.
Chilcott, Pte. A. J.
Child, Cpl. G. R.
Clark, Cpl. A. J.
Clark, Pte. L. S.
Clay, Cpl. A. T.
Cobb, Sgt. W. A.
Colley, Pte. G. L.
Collings, Pte. E. F.
Collins, Pte. H.
Cook, Pte. E. W.
Coombes, Pte. C. A.
Costerton, Sgt. H. P.
Cove, Pte. J. W. S.

Cowdy, Cpl. A.
Cowlishaw, Pte. A.
Cox, Pte. E.
Cox, Pte. H. N.
Cox, Pte. W. C.
Coxall, Pte. W. J.
Crocker, Pte. H. J.
Crofts, Sgt. P.
Croney, Pte. P. E.
Croney, Pte. S. P.
Crosby, Pte. H. E.
Crowther, Pte. H. J.

Dalton, L/Cpl. S. H.
Darlington, L/Cpl. S. J.
Dibley, Pte. J. W.
Dods, Cpl. J.
Dove, Pte. C. G.
Dowling, Cpl. H. E.

East, Pte. E. N.
Edwards, Pte. K. C.
Ellis, Sgt. W. E.
Elmy, Pte. W. C.
Etherington, Cpl. F. J.
Evans, Pte. F. W.

Fergusson, Pte. L. H. V.
Field, L/Cpl. S.
Finney, Pte. P. G.
Flack, Pte. J. E.
Flintan, Pte. P.
Fowkes, Pte. F. S.
Francis, Sgt. W. J.
Froude, Pte. W. J.
Fulker, Pte. S. L.

Gambling, Pte. H. J.
Gates, Pte. C. W.
George, Cpl. F. B.
Gibson, L/Cpl. W. J.
Ginn, Pte. A. W.
Godfrey, Pte. E. C.
Goodman, Pte. W. C. J.
Gosden, Pte. P. P.
Gould, Pte. S. G.
Griffiths, Pte. D. H.
Grinsell, Pte. C. H. J.

Hadingham, L/Cpl. H. R.
Haire, L/Cpl. N. E.
Haire, Pte. W. H.

Hall, Pte. J. M.
Harding, Cpl. A. J.
Harris, Pte. E. A.
Harrison, Pte. K.
Hawkins, L/Cpl. S. J.
Hedges, Pte. J. F.
Hiddleston, Pte. S.
Hill, Pte. P. J.
Hitchens, Pte. A. E.
Hobbs, Pte. A. W.
Hodges, Sgt. N. J.
Hodges, Pte. R. W.
Holding, Pte. H. R.
Hoie, Pte. J. A.
Hopkins, Sgt. J. A.
Houlden, Pte. H.
Howe, Sgt. F. E.
Huckwell, Sgt. P. A. R.
Hudson, L/Cpl. J.
Humphrey, Pte. J.
Humphreys, Pte. H. C.
Hunt, L/Cpl. H. E.
Hunter, Pte. J. A.

Ingram, Pte. P. R. P.

Jenner, Pte. L. C. J.
Jervis, Sgt. D. M.
Johnson, Cpl. J. E.
Johnstone, L/Cpl. A.
Jones, Pte. A. E.
Jones, Pte. E. A.
Jones, Pte. H.
Joyce, L/Cpl. B.
Jupp, Cpl. E. J.

Kearnes, Sgt. F.
Kennard, Pte. H. C.
King, Pte. S. N.

Lake, Pte. C. E.
Lambert, Pte. D. P.
Lambert, L/Cpl. D. R.
Lawton, Pte. A. V.
Lindsley, Sgt. W. V.
Litchfield, Pte. C.

Mackie, Pte. I. E.
Marshall Pte. L. F.
Marshall, L/Cpl. R. V.
Matthews, Pte. E. W.
Mayor, Pte. D. B.
Mills, Pte. A.
Mogford, Pte. G. S. H.
Monk, Pte. R. C.
Moore, Pte. A. J
Moore, Pte. R. M.
Morgan, Pte. E. W.
Moxham, Pte. B. J.
Muir, L/Cpl. G. D.
Muir, Pte. G. L.
McCarthy, L/Cpl. F. J.
McClelland, C.Q.M.S. F. C., м.м.
MacDondald, Pte. J. P.

Neale, Pte. F. M.
Neave, Pte. H. J.

Nelson, Sgt. J. S.
Nicholls, Cpl. E. J.
Noble, Sgt. A. J.
Norris, L/Cpl. E. W. J.
North, L/Cpl. R.

Ogborn, Pte. L. J.
Older, L/Cpl. A. L.

Page, Pte. H.
Palmer, Cpl. H.
Patterson, Pte. C. H.
Pearce, Pte. E. F.
Peskett, L/Cpl. H. M.
Pidgeon, Pte. T. A.
Porter, Pte. C. D.
Powell, Pte. E. H.
Prankard, Pte. G. F.
Price, Pte. E. A.
Pugh, Pte. E. E.

Radford, Pte. J. E.
Ralph, L/Cpl. L.
Rawlins, Cpl. R. E.
Ray, Pte. J. H.
Reeve, Pte. S.
Revell, Pte. T. F.
Reynolds, Pte. N. T.
Richardson, Pte. P. E.
Riche, Pte. S. W.
Roberts, Pte. S. F. O.
Roddon, Pte. M. D.
Rose, L/Cpl. P.
Rouse, L/Cpl. F.
Roussiano, Pte. T.

Sales, Pte. S. R.
Sandwith, Pte. C. F.
Sayers, Pte. A. W.
Schofield, Pte. G. K.
Scott, C.S.M. J.
Sheppard, Pte. R. J.
Simcox, Pte. J.
Simmons, Cpl. W. V.
Skelton, Pte. D. A.
Skinner, Pte. S. J.
Slade, Pte. H. A.
Smart, L/Cpl. J. G.
Smith, L/Cpl. A. H.
Smith, Pte. C.
Smith, Pte. G. F. F.
Smith, Pte. V. H.
Smith, Pte. W. H.
Smithson, Pte. E. F.
Spedding, Pte. G.
Spooner, Pte. L. A.
Spratt, Pte. V. A.
Stephens, Sgt. S. F. H.
Stocks, Pte. L.
Stubbings, Pte. E. O.
Swaffield, L/Cpl. A. C.
Syer, Cpl. L. M.
Symonds, Pte. D.

Taylor, Pte. L. G.
Tredinnick, Pte. R. W.

58TH SURREY HOME GUARD

Tribe, L/Cpl. T.
Trigg, Pte. C. B.
Trigg, Pte. R. D.
Trill, L/Cpl. J. C.
Trott, Pte. G. H.
Tugwell, Pte. J. W.
Vipond, Pte. A. E.
Wade, Pte. P. R
Wadham, L/Cpl. P.
Walker, Pte. P. R.
Wallis, Cpl. D. T.
Wallworth, Pte. R. R.
Wardill, Sgt. F. C.
Warner, Pte. F. R.
Warren, Pte. W. C.
Webb, Cpl. E. G.

Webb, Pte. J. Y.
Webb, Pte. R. F.
Webster, Pte. R. G.
Wellard, Pte. C. J.
Westwood, L/Cpl. D. F.
Wheatley, Pte. E. H.
Wheatley, Pte. G. A.
Wheeler, Pte. F.
White, Pte. C. H.
Williams, Pte. V. A.
Wilson, Sgt. G. S.
Windust, Pte. R. H.
Worley, Pte. R. E.
Woollacott, Pte. H. S.
Young, Cpl. C. F.
Young, Pte. W. J. W.

'B' COMPANY

Abbott, Pte. G. E.
Abel, Pte. W. E.
Affleck, Pte. R. J.
Aldred, Pte. T. P.
Amery, L/Cpl. C. R.
Angior, Pte. G. J.
Bailey, Pte. D. C.
Bailey, Pte. F. W.
Bailey, Pte. P. W.
Baker, Pte. J. M.
Baker, Pte. V. G.
Bancroft, Pte. A. J.
Banks, Pte. D. W.
Barlow, Pte. W. G.
Barnes, L/Cpl. E. W.
Barnes, Pte. H. H.
Batstone, Sgt. R. K.
Battle, Pte. E. W.
Battle, Pte. W. J.
Baudhuin, Pte. A. J.
Bayley, Pte. G. S.
Bayliss, Pte. H.
Beamish, L/Cpl. W. F.
Bentley, Pte. R.
Berard, Pte. M. J. P. J.
Berry, Pte. H.
Bevington, Pte. G. E.
Bibby, Pte. H.
Bird, L/Cpl. S. F.
Bishop, Cpl. L. E.
Bishop, Pte. W. S.
Bloxham, Pte. L. R.
Booth, Pte. R. F. C.
Bourne, Pte. H.
Bridgen, Cpl. H. E., M.M.
Brockes, Pte. R. T.
Brown, Pte. F. H.
Brown, Pte. H. E. A.
Brown, Pte. T.
Brown, Pte. W.
Brown, Pte. W. D.
Buchanan, Pte. T. Mc.
Bunclark, Pte. C. H.

Burroughs, Pte. A. O.
Bushell, Pte. D. N.

Canning, Pte. L. A.
Catterson, Pte. A. R.
Chamberlain, Pte. L. A.
Chamberlayne, Sgt. G. H.
Clarke, Pte. A. P.
Clarke, L/Cpl. S. J.
Chinn, Pte. T. E.
Clover, Sgt. G. W.
Clubb, Pte. D. A.
Coe, C.Q.M.S. H. F.
Cohen, Pte. S.
Coldman, L/Cpl. S. E.
Cook, Pte. A. E.
Cook, Pte. A. W.
Cousins, L/Cpl. R.
Craig, Pte. W. G.
Croager, Pte. J.
Crocker, Sgt. W. A.
Crofts, Pte. K. L.
Crump, Sgt. C. A., M.C.
Crutch, Pte. H. W.
Currie, Pte. J.
Curwain, Cpl. R. D.

Dalby, Pte. W. T.
Daniels, Pte. C. G.
Davies, Pte. D. N.
Davies, Pte. R. M.
Davies, Pte. W. R., M.M.
Dean, Pte. F.
Derrick, Pte. P.
Deubert, Pte. L. S.
Dolloway, Pte. H. S.
Douthwaite, Pte. J. L.
Doy, Pte. S. A. E.

Ebbutt, L/Cpl. F. C.
Ede, Sgt. R.
Edwards, Cpl. W. H.
Eillingham, Cpl. R. E. L.
Elliott, Pte. C. P.
Ellis, Cpl. A. A.

Ellis, Pte. J. E.
Ellis, Pte. J. W. E.
England, Pte. F.
Engleburtt, Sgt. J. F.
Fisher, Sgt. A. S.
Floyd, Pte. H. B.
Folland, Sgt. V. E.
Francis, Pte. R. G.
Freeland, L/Cpl. J. G.
Frewing, L/Cpl. D. A.
Frewing, Pte. H. W.
Fuller, Pte. E.
Furniss, Pte. E. J.
Gayler, Pte. E. A.
Gladwin, Pte. W. B. F.
Goodey, Pte. G.
Goodwin, Pte. H. T.
Gorton, Pte. C. G.
Gotts, Pte. L. G.
Gould, Cpl. E. D.
Gray, Pte. P.
Green, Sgt. A. S.
Griffiths, Sgt. T. H.
Grinstead, L/Cpl. A., M.M.
Groves, L/Cpl. J. W. M.
Hale, Pte. E. W.
Hall, Pte. E. W.
Hall, Pte. J.
Hambidge, Pte. W. G.
Hamilton, Pte. I. J.
Hammond, Pte. J. W.
Harman, Sgt. A. J., M.C.
Harmer, Pte. V. F.
Hart, L/Cpl. J. R.
Harvey, Cpl. F. J.
Harvey-Jones, Pte. R.
Hatton, Pte. W. J.
de Heger, Pte. V. D.
Henderson, Sgt. L. E.
Hepworth, Sgt. E.
Heron, Pte. D.
Hibberd, Pte. P.
Hicks, Pte. E. G.
Hitchcock, Cpl. F. T.
Holbrook, Pte. G. J.
Horton, Pte. G. T.
Hough, Pte. C. J.
Houghton, Cpl. C.
Howard, Pte. C. B.
Howis, Pte. J. A. J.
Hudson, Pte. R. H.
Hussey, Pte. L. C.
Ingram, Sgt. E. P.
Irving, Sgt. A.
Ives, Pte. L. W.
Jacques, Pte. N. C.
Jackson, Pte. R. M.
Jenkyns, L/Cpl. G. H.
Johnson, Pte. G. F.
Jones, L/Cpl. D. T., D.C.M.
Justice, Pte. D. J.

Kearsey, Pte. C. F. W.
Kemp, Cpl. J. C.
Kent, L/Cpl. H. S.
Lamb, Cpl. A. W. J.
Lambert, Pte. W. E.
Langmaid, Pte. S. J.
Leckie, Pte. J. M.
Leedham, Pte. C. H.
Lees, Cpl. R.
Leslie-Smith, Pte. R.
Light, Pte. G. S.
Lines, Pte. A. G. C.
Linley, Pte. H. G.
Little, Pte. W. J.
Lomas, Pte. A. H.
Long, Pte. V. G. H.
Lonsdale, Pte. W.
Lufkin, Pte. A. F.
Mackins, Pte. W. C.
Mallam, Pte. A.
Markwick, Pte. A. W.
Marsh, Cpl. F. L.
Marshall, Pte. J.
Marshall, Pte. R. J.
Marston, Pte. R. L.
Mason, Cpl. R. J.
Mayger, L/Cpl. F. R.
Minshull, Cpl. E. F.
Mitchell, Pte. C., M.C.
Morris, L/Cpl. E. L.
Morris, Cpl. R. W.
Mountain, Cpl. J. F.
Muckleston, Pte. H. P.
Mundy, Pte. E. S.
Munford, Pte. J. E.
McClean, Pte. W. E.
McCloy, Pte. W. E.
McDonald, L/Cpl. D. H.
Mackintosh, Sgt. S. D.
Macleod, L/Cpl. A. J. C.
Macquire, Pte. O. E.
McRae, Pte. R. H.
Neale, Pte. W.
Nelson, Cpl. H. G., M.C.
New, Pte. M. B.
Newman, Cpl. H. H.
Newton, Pte. J.
Nicholson, L/Cpl. E. R.
Norman, Pte. F. M.
North, Pte. F. St. J.
Ockenden, C.S.M. A. E. A.
Osborne, Pte. C. B.
Parker, Pte. F.
Parker, Sgt. S. J., M.C., D.C.M.
Parson, Pte. R. J. C.
Pascall, Cpl. S. W.
Pearson, L/Cpl. R. S., M.M.
Phillips, Pte. A. F.
Phillips, Sgt. H. N.
Plowman, Pte. H.
Powles-Hunt, Pte. R. G.

58TH SURREY HOME GUARD

Price, Cpl. R .S.
Pringle, Pte. A. V.
Quarterman, Sgt. J. T.
Rabson, Pte. H. G.
Ramsey, Pte. E. J.
Rendell, Pte. R. D.
Rennie, Sgt. F. A., M.M.
Rich, Pte. J. R.
Richardson, Pte. S. H.
Rimmer, L/Cpl. E. J.
Robertson, L/Cpl. G. A.
Ronicle, Pte. F.
Rudolph, Pte. H. B.
Rutt, Pte. H. L.
Sabey, Pte. E. L. S.
Sandwell, Cpl. E. F. L.
Sanwell, Pte. G. W.
Sapsford, Pte. S. A.
Sayers, Pte. E. A.
Schafer, Pte. P. O.
Scott, Sgt. J. D.
Scrivener, Pte. S. W.
Shirley, Pte. S. C.
Shoemack, Pte. E., M.M.
Simmons, Cpl. R. C.
Skelton, L/Cpl. G.
Skelton, Pte. H. V.
Skertchly, Pte. N. H.
Smith, Pte. C. A.
Smith, Pte. C. E.
Smith, Cpl. D.
Smith, Pte. E. J.
Smith, Pte. H. A.
Snape, Pte. J. A.
Snow, Pte. H. C.
Sommer, L/Cpl. J.
Southgate, Pte. C. G.
Spikins, L/Cpl. E. G.
Spruyt, L/Cpl. N. J. P.
Steddall, Pte. G. E.
Stelfox, Cpl. A. E.

Stuckes, Pte. R. C.
Surridge, Pte. W. C.
Swain, Pte. C. J.
Tarver, Pte. A. A.
Taylor, Pte. G. E.
Terry, Pte. H. A.
Thomson, Cpl. R. M.
Thornhill, Pte. H. B.
Tombleson, Pte. C.
Trenholme, Pte. K. M.
Trowbridge, Pte. M. E. O'K.
Turner, L/Cpl. K. R.
Tyrrell, Pte. J. E.
Vidler, L/Cpl. T.
Walker, Sgt. F. B.
Wall, Pte. H. T.
Walters, Pte. R. T.
Walton, Pte. H. L. F.
Webb, Pte. C. T. M.
Wellington, Pte. H. F.
Whalley, Pte. F. K.
Wheeler, Pte. L. F.
White, L/Cpl. W. D.
Whittle, Pte. F., M.M.
Wignall, L/Cpl. E. W.
Willcocks, L/Cpl. W. H.
Williamson, Pte. G. A. R.
Williamson, Pte. R.
Wilson, Pte. W. A.
Withers, Pte. R. R. J.
Wood, Pte. R. G.
Wood, Sgt. T. D.
Wright, Pte. A. J.
Wright, Pte. F. O.
Wright, Pte. I. A.
Wright, Pte. L. G.
Wright, Pte. W. A.
Wyllie, Cpl. A. G.
Young, Pte. J. S., M.C.
Zimmerman, L/Cpl. F.

'C' COMPANY

Acott, Pte. H. J.
Akehurst, L/Cpl. J. P.
Alexander, Pte. S. S.
Allison, Pte. J.
Apsee, L/Cpl. L. F.
Ardley, L/Cpl. H. A.
Ash, Pte. G. W.
Ashurst, Pte. P.
Atkins, Pte. E. J.
Atkins, L/Cpl. J. T.
Avis, L/Cpl. R. W. E.
Avisson, Pte. A. F.
Axford, Sgt. H. C.
Ayling, Sgt. C. H.
Bainbridge, Pte. A. H. J.
Baker, Pte. W. J.
Baldwin, Pte. A. E.
Banfield, Pte. F. S.

Barnes, Pte. J. W.
Batchelor, Pte. E. W.
Beacham, Pte. J. F.
Beadell, Pte. W. G.
Bean, Cpl. C. G.
Bell, Pte. B. E.
Bell, Pte. P. G.
Bell, Pte. T. C.
Bell, Pte. W.
Belton, Pte. H. W.
Billyard, Pte. C. E.
Bithell, Pte. F. P.
Blake, Pte. E. C.
Boniface, Pte. G. H.
Borsley, Pte. L. R.
Bostel, Pte. F. A.
Bowers, Pte. P. B.
Bradshaw, Pte. H. C.

Bridgwater, Pte. B. C.
Brooks, Pte. R. A.
Brown, Sgt. S. G.
Bullock, Pte. A. W.
Bundell, Pte. H. J.
Bushell, Pte. A. J.
Butterworth, Pte. B.
Campbell, Pte. A. B.
Carter, Pte. H. J.
Carver, Pte. J. T.
Casbolt, Pte. G. D.
Chadwick, Pte. G.
Chambers, Pte. G. S.
Charlton, Pte. C. L.
Cheal, Pte. W. H.
Church, Pte. A. G.
Clark, Pte. P. L.
Clarke, Pte. H. F.
Close, Pte. W. A.
Clover, Pte. K. R.
Codling, L/Cpl. R. G.
Collett, L/Cpl. A. E.
Cook, Pte. J. F.
Cooke, Pte. C. H.
Cooke, L/Cpl. E.
Cooke, Pte. E.
Cooke, Pte. P. J.
Cooper, Pte. E. H.
Cooperstein, Pte. J. M.
Corkett, Pte. R. H.
Cowen, Pte. C. H.
Cray, Pte. F. W.
Creal, Pte. H. W.
Crippen, Pte. E. A. G.
Crisp, L/Cpl. A. J.
Crone, Pte. H. G.
Cross, Pte. H. C.
Cross, Pte. W. A.
Curry, Pte. W.

Dale, Pte. A. C.
Dale, Pte. P. W.
Dance, Pte. E.
Davey, Pte. F.
Davey, Pte. J.
Davis, Sgt. D. A.
Davison, Sgt. B. E. A.
Dawe, Pte. L. R.
Deeks, Pte. R. C.
Denny, L/Cpl. F. H.
Dobb, Sgt. R. A.
Doe, Pte. A.
Douch, Pte. B. R.
Douglas, Pte. A. A.
Dulake, Pte. G. T.

Eales, Pte. R. G.
Edwards, Cpl. A. G.
Elkins, Pte. A. J.
Elkins, L/Cpl. L. A.
Elson, Pte. D. C.
Endacott, Pte. E. E.
Endersby, Pte. A. H.
Enright, Pte. P. D.

Evans, Pte. F.
Feldon, L/Cpl. R. G.
Felton, Cpl. F.
Finch, Pte. W. G.
Fletcher, Pte. H. J.
Foord, Pte. G. H.
Forcey, Pte. R. C.
Ford, Cpl. G. W.
Ford, L/Cpl. H. H. A.
Fox, Pte. W. T. P.
Francis, Pte. R.
Franklin, Pte. F. G.
Freeborn, Pte. E. E.
Freeman, Pte. L. C.
Fuller, Cpl. J. C. H.
Fuller, L/Cpl. P. W.

Gevers, Pte. P.
Ghent, Pte. F.
Gibbs, Pte. W.
Gifford, Cpl. G. C.
Gill, Pte. A. T.
Gill, Pte. R. H.
Gloyn, Pte. J. G.
Goodchild, L/Cpl. E. A.
Gooding, Pte. A. N.
Goodman, Cpl. E. H.
Gowar, Pte. J. E.
Gowen, Cpl. L. C.
Graham, Pte. S. E. M.
Grimston, Sgt. S. E.

Hacker, Pte. H.
Hackett, Pte. F. S.
Haigh, Pte. J. S.
Halls, Pte. P. M.
Hancock, Pte. C. P.
Harris, Pte. F.
Harris, Pte. P. M.
Harryman, Cpl. W. E.
Harwood, Pte. L. F.
Haynes, Pte. T. W.
Haywood, Pte. T. A.
Hearsey, Pte. S. F.
Heasman, L/Cpl. M.
Heller, Cpl. H. C. E.
Henderson, Pte. H.
Herring, Pte. G. W.
Herron, Pte. J. H. E.
Hicks, Pte. R. E. E.
Hill, Pte. A. W.
Hill, L/Cpl. S. R.
Hillier, Pte. M. W.
Hinton, Pte. A. F. W.
Hobart, Pte. A. E.
Hollobone, Cpl. H. E. W
Holmes, Pte. F. S.
Holmes, Pte. J. P.
Homewood, Pte. A. G.
Hopkins, Pte. C. J.
Howard, Pte. W. L.
Howitt, Pte. E. A. G.
Humphrey, Pte. A. J.
Humphreys, Cpl. E. R.

58TH SURREY HOME GUARD

Humphris, Pte. N. K.
Hunt, Pte. R. P.
Hunter, Pte. L. W.
Hurst, Cpl. C. H.
Hyde, Pte. J. P.
Ireland, Pte. R. J. J.
Jack, Pte. G. W.
Jacob, Sgt. W. E.
James, C.S.M. M. H.
James, Pte. P. T.
Jeffrey, Pte. E. D.
Johnson, Pte. W. R.
Jones, Pte. A.
Jones, Pte. M. S. C.
Josling, Pte. H. L.
Kemp, Pte. H. C.
Kench, Cpl. R. O.
Kerman, Pte. J.
Kerr, Pte. A. W.
Kilminster, Pte. A. W.
King, Pte. E.
King, Cpl. H. S.
Latham, Pte. R. C.
Lee, Sgt. T. V.
Legg, Pte. E. M.
Leggett, Pte. J. D.
Lemmon, Pte. W. D.
Lenton, Pte. H.
Lewis, Pte. F.
Lloyd, Sgt. R. A. H.
Loach, Pte. A. C.
Loveland, Pte. S. H. J.
Lush, Pte. W. J.

Martin, Sgt. A. E.
Martin, Pte. R.
Martingell, Pte. C. C.
Martingell, Pte. M.
Mash, Sgt, R. A.
Medhurst, Pte. C.
Metcalfe, Pte. F.
Middleton, Sgt. J. F.
Millard, Pte. R. F.
Mitcham, Pte. H. L.
Moakes, Pte. W. A.
Money, Pte. A.
Money, Pte. J.
Monk, Pte. R. J.
Monument, Pte. F. R.
Moody, Pte. N. C.
Moore, Pte. C. V.
Moore, Cpl. G. E.
Morton, L/Cpl. R. T.
Myers, Sgt. C.
McCallum, Cpl. W.
McMillan, Sgt. C. W.

Naylor, Sgt. H. E.
Neale, Pte. A. W.
Nichols, Cpl. A. W.

O'Neill, Pte. C. A.
Osterwalder, Pte. R. O.

Palmer, Pte. G. E.
Palmer, Pte. J.
Panton, Pte. W. M.
Parker, L/Cpl. G. A.
Parkes, Pte. R.
Parsons, Pte. W. H.
Paul, Pte. I.
Perry, Pte. A. L.
Pettet, L/Cpl. W. J.
Picksley, L/Cpl. C. W.
Pitchforth, L/Cpl. A. E. J.
Pitt, Sgt. S. R.
Plummer, L/Cpl. M. S.
Pollitt, L/Cpl. E. H.
Pope, Cpl. E. M.
Potter, Pte. W. J.
Potts, Pte. G. H.
Price, Sgt. J.
Pritchard, Pte. J. H.

Radford, Pte. W. A.
Raffield, Pte. T. G. W.
Raindle, Sgt. J. R.
Reed, Sgt. F. W.
Reeve, Pte. B.
Richards, L/Cpl. A. E.
Richford, Cpl. A. T.
Richmond, Pte. G. W.
Roberts, Pte. E. L.
Roberts, Pte. F. R.
Rogers, Pte. F.
Ronalds, L/Cpl. D. A.
Rudling, Pte. F. P.
Russell, Pte. P. G.

Sales, Pte. J. L.
Sales, Sgt. J. S.
Salmon, Pte. R. D.
Salmon, Pte. W. L.
Sankey, L/Cpl. L. G.
Savage, C.Q.M.S. F. A.
Savage, Pte. J. E.
Scarsbrook, Sgt. L. T.
Scott, Pte. J.
Sears, Pte. A. N.
Setter, Pte. L. J. M.
Shaw, Pte. N. C.
Shearman, Cpl. C.
Shoesmith, Pte. J. C.
Side, Pte. R. D.
Skeel, Pte. R. G.
Smith, Pte. E.
Smith, L/Cpl. G. S.
Smith, L/Cpl. H. A.
Smith, Pte. H. V.
Smith, Cpl. S. R.
Starnes, Pte. S. E.
Stephens, Pte. T. J.
Stephenson, Pte. A.
Stone, Pte. H. C.
Stride, Pte. E. R.
Stride, Pte. F. M.
Summerhayes, Pte. M. H.
Sumner, L/Cpl. L. W.

Swan, Cpl. E. N.
Sweet, Pte. G. W.
Tasker, Pte. A. W.
Tattersall, L/Cpl. P. R.
Taylor, Pte. A.
Terry, Pte. A. L.
Thomson, Pte. H.
Thorpe, Pte. E. W. W.
Thurgood, Pte. H. F. A.
Till, Pte. C. H.
Townsend, Cpl. W.
Trent, Pte. H. J.
Tubman, Pte. C. F.
Turner, Pte. W. T.
Venters, Pte. J.
Vincent, L/Cpl. F. W.
Vine, Pte. E. R.
Voss, Pte. H. A.
Ware, L/Cpl. J.
Warren, Pte. C. R.
Warren, Pte. T. E.
Wastell, Pte. F.
Watts, Pte. F. J. F.

Weatherley, Pte. J. H.
Weatherstone, Pte. L. S.
Webb, Pte. R. G.
Webb, Pte. W. W.
Welham, Pte. R. F.
Wellman, Pte. L. C.
Westley, Pte. R. A. V.
Westley, Pte. R. J.
Wheeldon, Pte. E.
Wheeler, Cpl. P. C.
White, L/Cpl. J. W. F.
White, Sgt. R. C.
Wilders, Pte. B. P.
Wilkins, Pte. N. H.
Willcocks, Pte. F. R.
Williams, Pte. E. J.
Williamson, Sgt. L.
Wood, Pte. W.
Wood, Pte. W. A.
Woodman, Pte. G. H.
Woodruff, Pte. R. F. E.
Wooldridge, Pte. A. O. S.
Wright, Pte. H. C. G.
Younger, Pte. E. J.

'D' COMPANY

Abbey, Pte. D. W.
Allam, Pte. J. B.
Allan, Pte. A.
Allan, L/Cpl. K. D., M.C.
Allen, Pte. A. J.
Anderson, Pte. F. A.
Anwyl, Sgt. A.
Ashdown, Pte. H. J.
Austen, Cpl. R. R.
Avery, Pte. W.
Bailey, L/Cpl. A. A. F.
Baker, Pte. S. H.
Balls, Sgt. L.
Barger, Pte. A. A.
Barker, Pte. D. M.
Barker, C.S.M. M. W. H.
Barwick, Cpl. R. H.
Bassam, Pte. H. E. G.
Bassett, Pte. J. T.
Batten, L/Cpl. H. C.
Beadle, Pte. R. F.
Belton, Pte. S.
Bennett, Pte. B. J.
Beswick, Pte. A.
Berry, Pte. R. F.
Betchley, Pte. W.
Bichard, Pte. J. A.
Blatcher, Pte. D. G.
Booth, Pte. H.
Borer, L/Cpl. D. A.
Borer, Pte. P. K.
Bowers, Pte. C. W.
Bowser, Pte. P. H. G.
Boyce, Pte. P. E.
Bradnock, Pte. J. W.
Brandon, Pte. W. F.

Bridgland, Pte. F. J.
Briley, Pte. B.
Brown, L/Cpl. J. W.
Brownell, Pte. J. F.
Buckland, Pte. F. E.
Burgess, Pte. G. A.
Burson, Sgt. W. S.
Canfield, Pte. H.
Canfield, Pte. H. E.
Carpenter, Sgt. E.
Carter, Pte. R.
Chaperlin, Pte. W. C.
Causley, Sgt. W. R. P.
Chapman, L/Cpl. H. E.
Chick, Pte. P. S.
Child, Pte. A.
Chiles, Pte. A. B.
Chinn, Sgt. F. J.
Churly, Pte. W. J.
Clark, Sgt. H. M.
Clifford, Pte. H. W.
Collins, Sgt. A. H.
Collins, Cpl. R. H.
Cook, Pte. G. H.
Cook, Pte. P. A.
Cook, Pte. W. J.
Cousens, Pte. H. A.
Cox, Cpl. P. V., M.M.
Cracknell, Pte. H. P.
Cripps, L/Cpl. G. C. E.
Dargavel, L/Cpl. A. H. B.
Davies, Pte. A. L.
Davis, Pte. H. P. B.
Dawe, Pte. A. C. T.
Dennett, Pte. W.
Devonshire, Pte. E., M.M.

58TH SURREY HOME GUARD

Dibley, Pte. A. H. F.
Dooley, Pte. W.
Dowell, Pte. F.
Driscoll, Pte. J.
Dubois, Cpl. F. E. A.
Duley, Pte. W. J. A.
Dunn, Pte. J.
Eade, Pte. J. A.
Edwards, Pte. J.
Elliott, Pte. S. A.
Ellis, Cpl. H. S.
Ellis, Pte. R. H.
Emerson, L/Cpl. J.
Everett, Pte. G. P. P.
Farman, Pte. S. L.
Ferguson, Pte. G.
Ferguson, Pte. G. A.
Fishlock, Pte. N. J.
Fores, Pte. F. C.
Franklin, Pte. C. H.
Fuggle, Pte. A. J. T.
Gamper, L/Cpl. F. M.
Garwood, Cpl. E. E.
Gates, Pte. H. S.
Gibbons, Cpl. J. W.
Gillett, Pte. L. R.
Gillham, L/Cpl. P. J.
Gillies, Pte. J. W.
Gould, Pte. A. E.
Grant, Cpl. A. R.
Greenacre, Pte. G. A.
Griffiths, Sgt. A. G., M.C.
Hamborg, Pte. R. E. M.
Harman, Pte. J. A.
Harries, Pte. W. J.
Haselden, Pte. F. C.
Haywood, L/Cpl. P. F.
Heaton, Pte. A. G.
Hedges, Pte. S. V.
Hennen, Cpl. L. C. G.
Hicks, Pte. T. C.
Hill, Pte. C. L.
Hill, L/Cpl. L. C., M.M.
Hillier, Pte. A.
Hodgson, Pte. W.
Holdsworth, Sgt. J. E.
Holland, Pte. K. H.
Humphrey, Pte. A. H.
Humphreys, Pte. C.
Hyre, Pte. G. F.
Hurst, Pte. E. J.
Ikin, L/Cpl. W. P.
Jaques, Pte. G. E.
Jennings, L/Cpl. G. L.
Johns, Pte. T. D. G.
Johnson, C.Q.M.S. H. M., M.B.E.
Jupp, Pte. E.
Keeble, L/Cpl. H. L.
Keel, Pte. W. S.
King, Pte. C. T. S.

Kitchin, Pte. J. T.
Knight, Pte. A. S.
Lapworth, Pte. C.
Last, Cpl. W.
Lee, Pte. V. T.
Lewis, Pte. W. R. H.
Lingwood, L/Cpl. E. G.
Looby, Pte. J. W.
Lovelace, Pte. W. R.
Lovell, Pte. G.
Lowis, Pte. C. H.
Lynch, L/Cpl. J. J.
Mair, Cpl. J.
Marney, Cpl. A. W.
Marsh, Pte. K. T.
Mayes, Pte. F. S.
Meeke, Pte. C. W. O.
Mendham, Pte. A. G.
Monger, Pte. J. W.
Moore, Sgt. A. S.
Moore, Pte. E.
Moore, Sgt. I. L. L.
Morgan, Pte. F. H.
Mowles, Pte. J. H.
Mullaly, Pte. H. A.
Murray, Pte. L. R.
Murray, L/Cpl. W. J.
McBride, Pte. M. W.
McCabe, Pte. F.
McClean, Pte. L.
Macfarlane, L/Cpl. A. R.
McIntyre, L/Cpl. G. D. M.
Nelson, Pte. G. H.
Neville, Pte. C. E.
Newman, L/Cpl. H. N.
Norris, Pte. J.
Nutland, Cpl. C. J.
Oakley, Pte. G. T.
Oliver, Cpl. F. J.
Parker, L/Cpl. R. B.
Payne, Pte. A.
Pearce, Sgt. A. E.
Perry, Cpl. R. I.
Pickering, Pte. S.
Plumstead, Pte. D. W.
Poate, L/Cpl. A. J.
Pope, Pte. D.
Pratt, Pte. A. G.
Pudney, Cpl. G. H. C.
Putman, L/Cpl. G. W.
Ramsden, Pte. W. E.
Rayment, Cpl. C. G.
Read, Cpl. C. H.
Reynolds, Pte. A.
Reynolds, Pte. A. E.
Richards, Pte. C.
Richards, Pte. J.
Richmond, Cpl. C. A.
Rickman, Pte. A. A.
Rigby, L/Cpl. A.

Roberts, Pte. T.
Robinson, L/Cpl. K. W.
Rogers, Pte. R. T.
Russell, L/Cpl. R. E.
Sadd, Pte. G.
Sands, Pte. E. T.
Sattler, Sgt. A. F.
Scott, Pte. E. N.
Sharp, Cpl. H. J.
Silvester, Pte. F.
Simmonds, Sgt. S. F.
Sisk, Pte. J. G.
Smith, Cpl. H. A.
Smith, Cpl. J. E.
Smith, Pte. S. W.
Smith, Pte. W. E.
Smith, Cpl. W. H.
Solesbury, Pte. G. E.
Spence, Pte. T. A.
Stanbridge, Pte. H. C.
Stephens, Pte. J. M.
St. Pier, L/Cpl. N. F.
Street, Sgt. V. C.
Stuchberry, Cpl. E. R.
Sutton, Pte. C. W.

Sykes, Pte. H.
Tarrant, Pte. J. J.
Taylor, Pte. V. E. F.
Thomas, Pte. F. J.
Tidy, Pte. N.
Tidy, Pte. R. J.
Tomlin, Cpl. S.
Venner, Pte. V.
Vidler, Pte. W. H.
Vivian, Pte. J. A.
Voice, Pte. L. A.
Wallace, Pte. F.
Wallis, Pte. W. J. A.
Walmisley, Pte. D. M. F. W.
Wapling, Pte. D. C.
Ware, Sgt. J. H.
Watts, Pte. H. R.
Weatherley, Sgt. A. J.
Weller, Pte. S. J.
White, Pte. B. J.
White, Pte. D. G.
Wigmore, L/Cpl. A. S.
Williamson, Pte. H.

58TH SURREY HOME GUARD

BRITISH INDUSTRIAL SOLVENTS PLATOON

Adams, Pte. R. C.
Austin, Pte. J.
Baker, Pte. C. E.
Blackmun, Pte. T.
Boughton, Pte. H.
Broughton, Pte. P. W. J.
Brown, Pte. J. A.
Buchan, Pte. A. F. F.
Cash, Pte. W. E.
Draper, Pte. B. J.
Ferrier, Pte. J. W.
Fox, Pte. S. W. R.
Giles, Cpl. W. E.
Howard, Pte. F.
Huggins, Cpl. E.
James, Pte. T.
Miles, Pte. E.
Mitchell, Pte. R. C.
Mowat, Sgt. J. S.
Pearce, Pte. J. C.
Pepper, Pte. F. W.
Powell, L/Cpl. E.
Roberts, Pte. F.
Smith, Cpl. J. C.
Smith, Pte. W.
Steptoe, Cpl. A.
Stewart, Pte. R. G. J.
Sutton, Pte. A.
Sweetland, Pte. F.
Truelove, Pte. C.
Ward, Pte. E. G.
Winwright, Pte. W.
Wood, Pte. G. A. R.
Worrow, L/Cpl. G.

EAST SURREY WATER COMPANY PLATOON

Andrews, Pte. G.
Barker, Pte. D.
Brown, Pte. A. C.
Budgen, Sgt. J. H. M.
Canfield, Cpl. A. P.
Carter, Cpl. S.
Clargo, Pte. H. J.
Collins, Cpl. C.
Cooper, Pte. W. J.
Davey, Pte. A. W.
Davey, Pte. B. J.
Eke, Pte. H. A. D. J.
Gander, Cpl. H. G.
Gatward, L/Cpl. T.
Greenyer, Pte. E. W.
Jeffries, Pte. J. S.
Merridew, Pte. W.
Moore, Pte. F. H.
Pannell, Pte. C.
Perry, Sgt. A. F.
Riorden, Cpl. J.
Skilton, Pte. A. H.
Stephens, Pte. R.
Symmonds, Pte. A.
Tarran, Pte. E.
Wood, Pte. F. A.

BRITISH OVERSEAS AIRWAYS CORPORATION PLATOON

Adams, Pte. L. A. G.
Ball, Pte. H. C.
Choppin, Pte. S. G.
Crane, Pte. T. C.
Davies, L/Cpl. J.
Fox, Pte. C. W.
Gray, Pte. G.
Hancock, Pte. C. E.
Harris, Cpl. H. C.
Harrison, Cpl. W. C.
Hern, Pte. E. V.
Ingram, Pte. W. G.
Jakes, Pte. A. T.
Low, Pte. E. I.
Males, Cpl. S. W.
Miller, Pte. F. L.
Morris, Pte. O. R.
McLaurin, L/Cpl. C. E.
Powell, Pte. W.
Pringle, Pte. H. A.
Pullen, Pte. R.
Quigley, Pte. J. W.
Rickman, Pte. M.
Rodwell, Pte. P. G.
Spashett, L/Cpl. H. E.
Stewart, Pte. J. D.
Tout, Pte. S. A.
Verrell, Pte. G. H.
Wells, Pte. T.

Nominal Roll of Women Auxiliaries
at "Stand Down"—1st November, 1944

BATTALION HEADQUARTERS

Miss B. C. Newnham   Miss J. W. Raper

HEADQUARTERS COMPANY

Miss J. Orrell

'A' COMPANY

Mrs. B. Cox   Mrs. D. Davis
Mrs. J. Darlington   Miss D. Launchbury
Miss N. M. Darlington   Miss C. Young

'B' COMPANY

Mrs. D. Hall   Mrs. K. R. Higgins

'C' COMPANY

Mrs. L. M. Jenkins   Mrs. B. Monk

'D' COMPANY

Mrs. L. Chapman   Miss M. M. Ridley
Mrs. H. Day   Mrs. D. H. Scott
Mrs. E. M. Mayes

If France had had a Home Guard like you have in England, I doubt very much if the German invasion would have been a success.

>   Brig. Gen. MOHR,
>   American State Guard,
>   July, 1943.

www.ingramcontent.com/pod-product-compliance
Lightning Source LLC
Chambersburg PA
CBHW070548090426
42735CB00013B/3107